REFLECTION

By
RICHARD MOUSSEAU

MOOSE HIDE BOOKS
imprint of
MOOSE ENTERPRISE PUBLISHING
PRINCE TOWNSHIP
ONTARIO, CANADA

cover illustration by Richard Mousseau

REFLECTION
By Richard Mousseau
Copyright February 13, 2014

Published December 1, 2014

By

MOOSE HIDE BOOKS
imprint of
MOOSE ENTERPRISE PUBLISHING
684 WALLS ROAD
PRINCE TOWNSHIP
ONTARIO, CANADA
P6A 6K4
web site www.moosehidebooks.com

NO VENTURE UNATTAINABLE

ALL RIGHTS RESERVED, NO PART OF THIS BOOK MAY BE REPRODUCED WITHOUT THE WRITTEN PERMISSION FROM THIS PUBLISHER, THIS INCLUDES STORING IN RETRIEVAL SYSTEM OR TRANSMITTED IN ANY FORM BY ELECTRONIC MEANS, MECHANICAL, PHOTOCOPYING, RECORDING OR OTHER, WITHOUT THE WRITTEN PERMISSION FROM THIS PUBLISHER.

THIS BOOK IS A BIOGRAPHY OF HISTORY AND OF THE PERSONS THAT HAVE CREATED THE HISTORY. THIS COLLECTION OF STORIES IS TRUE TO THE BEST OF THE AUTHOR'S ABILITY IN RESEARCHING AND WRITING OF THE FACTS. THESE STORIES ARE GIVEN WITH THE GREATEST AMOUNT OF RESPECT TO THE PEOPLE AND OF HISTORY. THERE IS NO MALICIOUS INTENT TO THOSE LIVING OR TO THOSE DECEASED. CREATIVE NARRATIVE IS USED TO ENHANCE THE STORY LINES.

CREATED IN CANADA

SECOND EDITION

Library and Archives Canada Cataloguing in Publication

Mousseau, Richard E., author
        Reflection / Richard Mousseau.

Issued in print and electronic formats.
ISBN 978-1-927393-29-1 (pbk.). - -ISBN 978-1-927393-30-7(pdf)

        I. Title.

PS8576.0977R43 2014-11-27   C813'.54   C2014-906609-0
                                                             C2014-906610-4

DEDICATION IN REMEMBRANCE

Mother, Georgette and Father, Fernand and to those that have
intertwined through life.

Reflection is what one's self sees in the rippling surface of
passing time.

What others' may recall of an author's travel through life is
debatable.

Words written down for posterity define an existence.

REFLECTION

1

Expectations of what was to be seen reflecting off of the smooth surface of the water trough was not to be. Clear blue-green water, filled to the brim of the cast iron claw footed bathtub adapted to be an animal water trough, clearly showed an aged face of a man mystified by a personal image. Hints of specific features were reminiscent of Father's, the family's inherited nose, dad's black eyes in furrowed brows and even Mother's hidden silent humour.

Where had the years gone? Brows furrowed and clouding orbs peered through slits of eye lids in an attempt to view the years displaying events hovering over a green pasture. Bits of recalled memories drift in and out of the mind's eye, though not in chronicle order. Dates and years as mixed up as the faces of people at various stages of life. Faces were familiar though names were difficult to recall. Dates, years and ages were non existent. The stories were most prevalent, most vivid with minute details and background facts connected to others and their stories. The man had accepted long ago that it was fruitless to try to memorize ages, telephone numbers, addresses, birth dates and every calendar listing that most people easily recite. Placing dates to stories or trying to place a story in a chronicle order of happening is a waste of time. All stories happened yesterday, last year or just a time back.

Sixty years has lapsed and the man has adapted, learned, became successful, according to his own definition of success. Rich, no. Famous, no. Poor, no. He is just an every day average person. Six decades of hiding a learning disability is unique, a triumph and in a way a success story. Not a shared success story that requires a reward, nor an acknowledgement nor a need to publicly publish, rather self pride. In no way had he purposely tried to hide facts, or fool others, nor cheat in order to advance. A self admiration existed for the ability of adapting by figuring out alternate ways to learn and arrive at the same outcome that others achieve.

Studying the reflection in the cool water drawn up from a hundred and fifty feet below the earth's surface, he did not see any indication of a learning disability. That word, 'disability' he dislikes. A label, if required, he would say is just a learning hindrance. Maybe a hiccup in the thought process, a slight hindrance when computing the visual placement of letters and numbers in incorrect positions, and the memorization or calculations of facts.

Undoubtedly others have more severe learning roadblocks and difficulties. They are graded on the normalcy scale. Who makes the rules of normalcy? Those who self-proclaim to be normal, that is who. Ask any person with a hindrance and a reply will be, 'I am normal, because this is the way I was created.' Those who are of the majority of normalcy and suddenly suffer a hiccup in the learning process will strive to adapt to be normal within their limited abilities.

From the peripheral of view a bantam chicken pecked at the ground. Turning slightly, the man studied the puffy chicken covered in rusty coloured feathers from beak to toe nails. Well, not quite. Interested in a plump ant dashing between grass blades, the chicken aptly known as Hop-along hobbled over and pecked with success. Did Hop-along realize its' own disability? Missing the claw foot up to the first joint of the right leg, it would step with the assumption that the foot was there then slump down onto the peg leg. Two winters had come and melted away since the foot was lost. This should have been plenty of lapsed time for a chicken's brain to realize that the foot was gone. Yet, continuously the leg would rise, reach forward and hover an inch above the ground. An inch of space occurred where Hop-along expected the foot to be in order to support the step. Nope, the peg leg dropped, the leg making an imaginary second try then making contact with the ground. Repeated sequences occurred across the pasture. Hop-along ate well and was a normal one-pound under a three pound vision of puffy feathers.

Two winters earlier, a cold spell arrived early. Being a young chicken, it possessed a mentality of all young creatures, a denial that they are immune to harm. While other chickens headed for the enclosed coop or huddled together for warmth, Hop-along perched with face into the wind, somewhat cocky with the display of rooster plumage fluttering enticingly. Hens of the brood neither paid attention, nor beckoned Hop-along an opportunity to cuddle in shared warmth.

Night descended quickly cloaking the farm yard in a blackness void of moon and star light. Specs of snow filtered through the wired pen inflicting irritating pelting. More of a nuisance, rather acceptable compared to the nuisance of Northern Ontario mosquitoes and blood sucking females of the species. Hop-along's first spring of birth came with the introduction of the Genus, 'Humungus–Northern–vampira–

insectus'. Experience was first hand when just a day old chick. A Northern Ontario Humungus dove from above and knocked it off its unsteady claws. Undoubtedly a vivid and lasting introduction into the world of variety.

Hop-along's first introduction to snow was not all that bad, an interesting anomaly of the weather. Settled on its' perch, a roost position adapted by evolution, the species, 'Gallus gallus Domesticus' settled down for the night. Now that the darkness had enveloped and night vision limited, Hop-along declined an attempt to move. Roosting is an intuitive defence application to sustain existence. Weasels, Fox and Owls would disagree based on their hunting success at night.

On 'Sanora's Siesta, Ranch' the owner provides a secure home where Gallus gallus Domesticus is out of reach of prowling predators. Accommodations are adequate when used. This night Hop-along experienced the unexpected assault of Mother Nature's weather. Pelting and mounting snow accumulation was new and interesting to the chicken though the declining temperature aggravated the fowl. An abundance of feathers underlined by a downy layer warded off the cold. Fluffing by quivering boosted the chicken form into a puff ball of trapped warm air pockets. Being a show chicken, a Bantam-Partridge-Cochin', Hop-along boasted downy feathers down legs and over claw toes. Quickly dropping temperatures on this late October night penetrated the enclosure to bite at exposed fleshy surfaces. Blood-filled claw toes turned dark red. By morning a whitish line rimmed the toes and first leg joint of Hop-along's right leg. Puffed up and coated in a layer of snow, Hop-along waited, anticipating the morning's sun, possible warmth of energizing rays to thaw the lowered body core temperature.

Seasonal changes always seem to occur instantly despite knowing of its' scheduled arrival. And always the farm is not ready. Projects are not completed. Livestock is not ready to adapt and Ed scrambles to comply with the abrupt change. Fall procedures instantly become winter chores. Lying in the Queen-size bed alone, Ed stretches and tenses legs and back muscles in an effort to counter the inevitable symptoms of age. When did the body loose its' growth of youth? When did the decline begin? At what age does the uphill climb of anticipation, hope and wonder become the tumble down the slope toward the swamp of vegetating years and leisure time to reminisce of a life's adventure of the climb?

'The golden years!?' The person that coined this phrase must be in mental denial. The saying and meaning is crap. Aches and pains, slower movements and lacking energy amounts daily on a man that has laboured throughout life. Applying medications for aches and pains and swallowing the appropriate pill for the assumed aliment at the right time can be therapeutic when accomplished correctly. They say that, 'practise makes perfect'. True, and as Ed has experienced a logical thinking mind is also an asset.

Standing naked after a warm shower at the end of a hard day, Ed viewed the old body in the steamed mirror. The human mind does not age memories in the same way that a body does. A mind's expectation is of a young, muscle rippled form and not the wrinkled flabby skin and body hair turning grey. Upon viewing, Ed accepted the changes. Most changes had not been too extreme.

Evenly greying hair cover the head, though thinning at a slowly receding forehead hairline. Hair retention came from Father's Mother's side of the family where the men carried full heads of hair well into their seventies. It seemed that the elder sons retained full covering.

Unlike Ed's two younger brothers who sport full top of the head baldness which began to form in their late thirties. They inherited the hair loss gene from Mother's Father's side. Both brothers gained increasing weight with each aging year and bounced around the two hundred pound balance point on the medical scale.

They are bald, heavy in weight and in the height range of five-foot nine-inches and they are married with children and grandchildren? So why do they have the rewards of a family life? Ed's weight has only changed by twenty pounds from one hundred and sixty pounds at age sixteen to one hundred and eighty pounds on a six-foot one inch frame at sixty years of age. Unmarried, he has no children and no prospects of even winning the odds of receiving grandchildren from a produced child.

Checking for extreme sagging, Ed noted that his butt was still prime roast in caricature. What woman would turn sustained quality down? Though opportunity was presented and interaction experienced, women never lingered, never inclined to stay. Was the situation too safe, too mundane? There was never a clear understanding of why? Interpretation was a conclusion that each woman was searching for more. They wanted more of what? Knowing of the eventual men they settled with and their state of affairs and off-spring, Ed assumed that he could have been that man of selection. Then again he was spared from the hidden downfalls of those couplings. Financial woes, possible bickering, unruly children and all of the other negative ingredients one can list could have been his burdens. What of the wonderful moments? Those can be craved though have not and will not be experienced.

Animals are social creatures and can and do exchange affection, communication and depend upon a human and in response a human accepts and offers the same in exchange. Some people may assume that a farmer or rancher must be hard worn and deal with domesticated animals as a product. This is untrue. Often Ed has scolded a nuisance animal and shed a tear and sleepless nights when an animal is hurt or death draws the essence of the creature away.

Reaching into the pen to inspect Hop-along's predicament of a frozen claw, Ed sensed fright. An odd screech informed fellow chickens of impending infliction. All animals react to pursuit and handling. Hop-along's injury could have been inflicting constant pain. Once retaining a hold and cradled into an arm the chicken relaxed once sensing the security of the handling.

Gently a hand inspected the tenderness of healthy flesh and the cold hardness of the dead frozen limb. With a slight twist of the claw foot it severed cleanly off. A building apprehension of causing pain subsided in Ed's emotional mind when Hop-along did not physically react to the action, as if nature had performed the amputation with natural sequences. Ed breathed with relief.

Once placed on the ground the chicken displayed mixed reactions, somewhat in relief that the dead weight was eliminated, though anticipating a substance to be there when walking. Previously being reluctant to be handled, Hop-along no longer attempted to avoid being approached or handled. To be cradled in an arm and transported to the feeding grounds of the pasture, it truly relished. A bond of sorts was shared between Hop-along and Ed that did not exist between other chickens.

There was no essence of vanity in the way Ed inspected himself in the mirror. It was the same study in the same way he studies the tractor or plough or a fence post. Those checks of importance that qualifies the object for the job it is designed for.

Beauty is completely a different matter. A good tractor or a good horse is an object of beauty when viewed for its' shine and shimmer and firmness of structure. A tractor's fenders without dents, rust and paint of lustre glinting in the beholder's eye is Ed's interpretation of beauty. Often he has used the same guidelines when comparing a woman and a horse. Proportion of shape to suit the body and the way each holds a stance and struts, the strong and soft features of their face and their intense stare that shows inquisitiveness and trust, this is what Ed says is beauty. Unfortunately the success Ed has had is with the long companionship of horses. In hind thought, sharing years of mutual relationships, both horse and man have been most fortunate. The notion of experiencing a relationship with a woman is not totally disregarded.

Eyeing the figure reflecting in the mirror, Ed started from the feet and worked upward. Size ten feet, toe nails trimmed neatly with only one crooked small toe is surely acceptable feet for a woman to view. Legs stand sturdy with an evenly coated layer of sparse hair except for the lower calves that shine smoothly and are bald. Wool socks worn extensively throughout life pulled hairs free and polished the pale skin.

Thighs are strong, butt prime roast, belly a bit convex but not a pot belly except in the hibernating months of winter, and chest is all in place and not showing the sag of age. Very sparse hair on chest, though still a full head of hair, unlike a younger brother who sports a bald head and an over abundance of hair on chest and back. Typical of most farm men only the hands just past the wrist and a vee patch ending on the chest from the neck have the permanent tan that contrasts with the anemic pale colouring of the rest of the body.

Studying the reverse reflective face, Ed nodded acceptance of the proportioned features; brown eyes, slim nose hooked slightly to the right, short trimmed beard and moustache speckled with advancing grey. Pretty would be an exaggeration. Handsome with normalcy is a possibility. A six if Ed had to self rate on a scale of ten give or take a point five variable for whether a smile was offered or not. As a package why would a woman not lower her perfect man standards and accept Ed as is. Ed gestured to the mirrored reflection in an upturned questioning hand flourish. In an answer the spirited aspiration lowered its' head to stare below Ed's belly.

Do women look and judge a man and future relationship on the structure and size of the male appendage? When do they judge; at the inactive moment when the membrane is shrivelled by the cold or at the moment of arousal? No instance could be recalled when a woman had stood back and studied his anatomy or made a comment. Maybe the lack of a woman was the unspoken answer. Ego stated a ranking of nine point five, though accepting an eight. To be hung like a horse is suitable for horses. If the standard average of six inches still applied to the male anatomy of measurement then Ed qualified.

Physically Ed qualified in all categories yet here he stood, still single, still available, still seeking. Sure there are always other physical properties to add into the equation though all members of the species have them and this should not be a factor. Having showered after a long work day and having studied his form it was time to medicate the aliments acquired over time.

One pill for lactose intolerance, three small pills for migraine prevention, two larger ones to be taken only when experiencing an attack, cream for elbow tendonitis, hot cream for lower back dislocation and bruising, cream for an irritating hemorrhoid and glasses required for aging eye sight in order to select correct remedy for corresponding aliments.

A procedure is required along with pre-though of previous action and an ability to remember the planed procedure of the unique remedy for the corresponding aliment.

A lesson learned when one pill was taken for lactose intolerance were for migraines thus a migraine was not stopped and the three migraine pills tuned out to be for lactose thus instant diarrhea. The inflamed exhaust port further inflamed when residue from the hot cream applied to the back before the hemorrhoid cream came in contact with the tender flesh of the butt crevasse. The constant lingering exhaust flame could not be doused.

It is not that the mind is forgetting nor memory leaking out, it is that Ed has lived and has added on a few years of sucked-in information into the mind meaning that the brain is overloaded. A solution is to create a saying that will keep medication consumption under control. First; arrange medicine in order of importance and application from left to right on the medicine cabinet shelf and match it to the saying. One lactose pill before three small migraine pills and two large ones if three do not work, then cold cream before hot. Always!

2

Not being a father, Ed did not experience the wonder of creating and raising a child. Within the thoughts of others he would not experience the joys and heartaches associated with the complexities surrounding the growth of another human being. It is not that Ed did not attempt to create a child. There were women and engagements without preventative insemination protection. Playing with a fire-mentality was overruled by desire. Was the survival just luck, fate or a predetermined outcome by Ed's spiritual creator? As a hunter would comment on a shooter that misses a target, 'are you shooting blanks?' Ed does not know and never had an inclination to find out.

Yet, there are occasions when similarities are experienced that relate to human emotions of raising a child until grown and comes the time to leave the nest. Often a story is told of a knock sounding hollow on the door of a church, orphanage or a family home on a distant road off the beaten track, and when the door is opened a bundle is noticed emitting baby sounds. In the days of old the child would be raised without a need to search for the reasons or persons behind the abandonment. The child would be treated as belonging.

On an unusual spring night high winds delivered rain clouds from the south, building and lingering over the area. Farm animals had anticipated a change in the weather. Knowledge is ingrained in animals, in the manner of instinctively knowing directions, knowing of the safe vegetation to eat and forecasting the weather and then adapting. Ed did not look out of a window to witness the correct weather status, rather studied the farm animals' mannerisms in order to forecast the weather.

Want to know the direction of the wind? It is predetermined by which way a horse's rump is facing. In a light wind its' tail swishes gently side to side and over the rump to displace flies. When a strong wind is intent on building, its' tail is pressed tight to seal the rump cheeks and hangs steady between legs. Rain forecasting is determined by how a cow reclines. A bovine lays down with back and rump in the direction of the approaching weather front.

In the early afternoon as the sky darkened, Ed studied the chickens and pigeons to determine the night's condition. Flight excursions by the pigeons ended before six P.M.. They had decided to roost in the pigeon hanger and call it a day. Claghorn, the head rooster was the last to enter the hen house once satisfied that all hens were accounted for. Stillness descended over the farm. Ed pondered the various actions of the animals and concluded that a windy rain storm will be passing through and lasting all night. He himself finished up chores early and headed indoors.

A heavy blanket of rain continuously fell, driven by bursts of sixty mile an hour winds. Darkness descended three hours prior to a normal sunset of eight-fifteen P.M.. Sleeping soundly, soothed by rain musically tapping on the tin sheeted roof, Ed's eyes popped instantly open at eight-ten A.M. when an odd silence prevailed. Mother Nature turned the new day's light switch on and immediately the rain, wind and darkness vanished.

A faint memory of a warm body next to him also faded before Ed rolled legs out of bed. Bend, twist, rotate feet, roll head and stretch arms, Ed manipulated body parts to make sure all were in working order before rising to feet. Morning birds eagerly hopped along the water soaked ground, pecking at worms and earth bugs displaced by the slowly sinking water table.

Both farmer and animals were late risers on this day and moved slowly in pace with the lazy morning working its' way toward a warming outcome. Cows slowly rose and stretched, chickens raced to peck at an abundance of earth bugs, pigeons took flight and horses and goats rushed to meet Ed entering the gate. Anticipating treats, all tagged along nosing hands and checking pockets. Pacos, an old gelding, a cross of Clydesdale-Palomino-Hackney headed Ed between the shoulders with an encouragement for its' master to hustle faster. Crowding the horse rail five horses stretched necks. Behind them two cows waited. At the feed shed door four goats stretched necks towards hands offering sweet feed.

Once all were fed it was time for Ed to survey the farm and check for wind damage to structures and trees, washouts and possible flooding. When walking, the ground responded in a spongy action indicating a major saturation. The beaver ponds in the back South East corner would be filled with water and seeping over earthen dams. Inlet and outlet creeks would be full.

Ed pondered the thinking process of beavers. No matter how deep the pond water is, if more water is added and creeps to the top of the dams, the water mammals will busily work around the clock to top-up the dams. They never seem to be satisfied. Though during the dry spring and summer of nineteen . . ., Ed could not recall the date yet associated the year with the arrival of an old nineteen fifty-seven Ford eight end tractor, the beavers were content with ponds filled to the brim.

A creek from the west feeding the beaver ponds also fed a small drinking pond at the farm. From a distance Ed noticed the dark brown of silt coloured water backwashed into the pond. An odd object floated in the centre of the calm water. A fuzzy ball of grey-white-blue tinge may be Akida's play object. The neighbour's dog, a black and white bread mix of something, maybe retriever and terrier, is not fussy about toys. A true runner and superb squirrel and chipmunk tracker and catcher distinguished this dog's legacy.

If it is not Akida's toy then what? Wandering down to inspect the oddity, Ed checked out the swollen creek. From afar Akida noticed the man and decided to join him in an inspection tour of the farm. Upon reaching the pond at the same time, human and canine greeted with a pat on the head and a tail wag. With surprise curiosity four eyes stared at two eyes of a gosling inspecting the two-legged tall being and the four-legged short creature with a tilted head.

Use to seeing the domestic chickens, ducks and geese that wander the farm, Akida accepted the pond fowl as just another nuisance. To tell the truth, Akida was skittish of fowl and always skirted around when encountering them. Chipmunks and squirrels were Akida's prey of choice.

Ed held concern for the week-old gosling seemingly alone in the pond. Wild geese do visit the wet lands on and near the farm and a mating pair nest by the beaver pond though Ed did not notice the pair this year. It is conceivable that during the pelting rain and wind the gosling could easily be separated from its' parents and siblings and float away in the surging water flow. Fox and coyote care less of the weather. Their hunger supersedes the application of the elements. If foraging in the area the hunters could have forced the gosling to use the security of the water to keep the hunters at bay. Backwash would have carried the gosling into the farm pond.

An orphan had been dropped off on the farm's doorstep. Care is not easily given to a wild creature as it is to a domesticated animal. A hand on application should not be applied. A safe distance should be maintained so that a dependency upon the care giver is not imprinted. Even without physical contact there definitely is an emotional contact that Ed maintains exists.

Ed squinted and rubbed a hand over short cropped facial hair as the mind pondered the safety of the gosling, required food, loneliness and separation from kin. Life's learning is developed in a family unit, learning by observation, trial and error and correction by parents. Who would teach this little fellow? Would observations of the domestic animals be absorbed by the gosling?

Akida and Ed wandered off leaving the little fellow floating in the pond surrounded by inquisitive frogs rising to the water's surface. Throughout the day curiosity forced Ed to lift his head to glance toward the pond. There in the middle of the pond it floated, its' head bobbing, stretching and twisting when a sound or vision caught its' interest. With the same curiosity Akida would wander down to the pond, though would sit at a distance to observe.

This is Akida's cooling off pond, for after chasing squirrels and chipmunks a dip in the pond is required on a warm day. Though having chased several squirrels this morning it is as if Akida respected and understood the need to leave the gosling undisturbed. Akida watched while panting to cool off. Once cooled, off ran the young female dog for another squirrel chirp was heard.

By late afternoon the horses, cows and goats had visited the pond for drinking and noticed the new pond dweller and made their introductions. From distant pens and the upland pasture the chickens, ducks and geese made verbal calls. The domestic fowl did not venture to the pond. Not a peep was emitted from the gosling. No similar species of the geese population came searching for the lost gosling. For that matter Ed noted that no goose calls had been heard throughout the day, nor had he sighted flyovers.

Worried about the hunger that the gosling may be experiencing Ed placed a mound of grain and cracked corn at the edge of the pond before the last of the day's light dwindled. Dreams of concern would definitely trace through Ed's sleep.

The first thoughts of concern urging Ed to wake was to check on the gosling. Rushing away from the bed and even passing the washroom, though needing to pee, Ed went to the south patio doors. Lifting binoculars to sleep caked eyes he aimed the binoculars towards the pond. Akida was already there sitting at a distance watching the gosling walking at the pond's edge and pecking at bugs, grass and grain.

Having company of strange animals visiting the pond, the gosling seemed to accept their companionship. Hope was that the trauma of being lost and in a sense abandoned by parents and siblings the gosling is adapting and accepting of its' circumstances.

Little by little it wandered further a-field though always returned to the security of floating in the middle of the pond at night. Of all of the farm animals the gosling attached itself to Pacos and followed the big old gelding about. Odd is the only way to describe the mutual attachment. When the horse moved and big hairy feet stepped about the gosling followed with its web feet inches from the hooves, yet there was never stepping of big hooves on flat webbed feet. When Pacos lay down for an afternoon nap the gosling snoozed hear the long white tail swishing at pesky flies. Pacos was the only animal that would share grain with the gosling.

The gosling did not walk like a horse; it waddled so Ed applied the name of Waddles to the gosling. After a month Waddles had lost all of the gosling fuzziness of down feathers and replaced by the Canadian goose colours and forming feathers. Waddles felt at home and was treated as just another resident of the farm. Though seeing, hearing and knowing the location of the domestic geese, ducks and newly arrived turkeys, Waddles never ventured to that part of the farm, preferring to associate with Pacos, the other horses, cows and goats.

How does one communicate with animals and do they communicate among themselves? Obviously each species communicates in their species own language. Ed speaks all languages and by mimicking sounds is able to communicate. Do non related species communicate? Does a goat understand a horse, a cow of a horse, a horse of a turkey?

Waddles had not made a sound from day one despite hearing the domestic geese speaking a dialect similar to the wild geese version and even Ed's vocalisation of both. At any moment Ed expected Waddles to speak horse, after all Pacos and Waddles spent a good portion of the summer together. Pacos is a laid-back horse, nothing seems to bother the old boy and it does not complain much, and never vocalizes as often as the female horses.

A change of weather came in small hints in September with evenings cooling off as the sun set earlier each day. Animal coats began to add new hairs for their winter coats. Waddles' wings had reached full extensions and it was aware of them, often extending, stretching and flapping the four-foot span. Maturity had been reached and Waddles was full grown. Still no goose vocalizations sounded from its' throat and it did not attempt to fly. If being satisfied with regular meals and a place to call home then there is no need to complain with a vocalization. With wings extended it walked behind Pacos. When chased by Babo, the head bad goat, Waddles ran on floppy feet.

Concerned for Waddles, Ed decided to force the visitor to fly. Akida sat watching in bewilderment as Ed flapped arms and honked as he chased the goose about the pasture. Other animals scattered to the sidelines, upset at being disturbed from their munching. Waddles' flat feet bounced across the short pasture grass with toenails always making contact with the ground. Exhausted, Ed gave up and panted for breath. Waddles had not gained even a slight lift off and settled back into a waddling walk towards Pacos to continue a life as a horse.

With the change of weather in the fall comes the urge in animals and birds to prepare for winter. Mammals add an undercoat of hair to ward off the winter cold. Pacos even grows longer hair to form an odd looking moustache that covers its' upper lip, probably a gene hair growth from the Hackney breed of horse. Fowl and birds have added an under layer of down, those that stay to ward off the Northern Ontario winters in Canada. Migrating birds begin to make practice flights and gather into flocks. Northern geese begin to fly over on the Great Lakes flyway.

Waddles heard the geese call from above with an invitation for others to join the flock. Not knowing that it belonged to the species of Branta Canadensis Maxima it just turned an eye skyward to watch V's forming in a southward direction. Waddles had been fed and in a sustained fat and muscle ratio though had not developed the ability to fly, just wing stretching and flapping exercises. If unable or has no intension to fly then a cold snow bound environment will be an eye awakening existence.

An Indian summer of a warm spell occurred in October after the Canadian Thanksgiving, an indication that the last of the Northern group of geese would be taking flight. Far Northern geese had stopped to rest in local farmers' fields. A V of two hundred geese high above reduced the ability to sight details were on a non stop flight towards the Mississippi delta wintering grounds.

The end of the week introduced a cold change with winter wind low to the ground and high warm winds above. With the sun setting

18

earlier the farm animals were changing their feeding habits and hanging around the barn more often. Waddles had never ventured to the barn area and was left alone by the pond.

Something on this night of low and high clouds mixing and the sky above illuminated by a three-quarter an agitation irked Waddles. Resting on haunches its' head and neck bobbed and twisted and its' beak opening and closing without sound. Watching from the fence rail with a white straw hat pulled down tight Ed felt for the goose with a wanting to fetch the fowl and bring it to friends at the barn, or to scold it for not talking with the geese above nor even in attempting to fly.

Tall pine and tamarack trees on the south side of the pond and pasture swayed violently in the crossed winds. Ed's vocal honk of reassurance to let Waddles know he was close by became lost in the wind's roar. Waddles did twitch its' head towards the dark figure at the fence. Through the roar came whispers of honking instructions from the void of sky above the clouds. A main group of southbound geese were calling for local smaller groups to join up.

Waddles sprang to its' feet and danced in place and wings began to stretch and flap with an eagerness of doing something engrained. Flying south at this time of year is the ingrained urge, though Waddles had never flown, never lifted off of the ground. Maybe it would suffer vertigo.

From a farm field north of Ed's place a flock of geese took flight and replied with honking to the high flying flock. Cresting the north section of mixed growth of poplar and jack pine trees the flock rose. Waddles noticed and instinct said to follow. At a full run into the northeast cross wind Waddles flapped with its' legs striding and leaping with grace of a hurdler. The pasture was ending at a brush section and Waddles had not even lifted into flight.

Feet slapped at the ground and wings flapped, tail feathers spread to create a rudder and its' neck stretched arrow straight into the wind. On a wing and a prayer web feet slapped at the air. By a foot then a yard the goose gained height. Ten-feet then twenty-feet above the ground and still its web feet ran and contacted the branches of white pine knocking pine cones free to rain down for hungry chipmunks.

Ed cheered silently with clenched fists tightening with anxiety. A swallow and released stomach muscles followed the success of Waddles' reaching above the trees. Waddles banked and wavered in the cross wind and trailed behind the rising flock of geese. Darkness and clouds swallowed the rising flock.

Instinct turned the gosling that thought it was a horse into a Canadian goose, one of hundreds of others on a south bound odyssey. Concern filled Ed's mind as eyes tried to pick out shadows of geese climbing to join the main flock. Never having any training flights, nor building up stamina, would Waddles be able to keep up and reach warmer feeding grounds. If accepting the last position of the V and staying in the drag position then less energy would be wasted. Waddles may manage to keep up.

Over the following days Waddles was missed by Ed and even the animals' sensed the void. Throughout winter Ed wondered if Waddles had made it south, wondered if it was accepted and if it now realised it is a goose. When spring arrived and knowing of the timeframe of returning geese Ed searched the sky, often dropping what chore was being done and racing into the open when hearing honking. Domestic geese had tricked him several times then honked in laughter.

On a mundane day of doing nothing Ed sat leaning back on an old hay wagon staring skyward. High, high above a main flock headed directly north. From the main group a splinter flock descended. Local resident geese would splinter several times with pairs returning to familiar areas to mate and raise their new gaggle.

Out of nowhere a single goose flew wide of the group and dropped low over the pasture. Ed's eyes widened with anticipation. Could it be? In a blink the wings wavered and legs dropped as if walking on air. Could it be? The flock flew out of sight over the tall tree tops with the lone goose following with feet slapping at the air and at tree top branches in a hesitant pursuit. Could it be?

Could it be? Maybe it was Waddles just saying hello and a 'made it and thanks for taking me in'. Who says that man and creatures do not share affection? A moist eye accompanied a tightened throat. Ed hoped that the goose was Waddles, an orphan that he was able to help and now had found a place among Branta Canadensis Maxima.

3

Ed accepts being alone, a hermit of sorts, and a bachelor to use a word of description. Hell, Ed is an old man, living alone, a recluse off the beaten path of society where livestock is often treated as family. They get along well, sometimes!?

Where did humans come from, and how did mankind develop differently than other mammals, reptiles and all combinations in these headings, and including insects? Upon the structural study of each creature's anatomy and skeletal framing, all are similar. An ape's hand is similar to a man's hand. The rib cage of a man is similar to that of a whale's huge rib cage. A shark, a horse, a spider, a rabbit, a man, an elephant and a mouse each have virginal genitalia and penis though slightly different in shape and size all use their apparatus for the same purpose. If so similar in all traits then did the mass varieties originate from a singular cell?

The teaching of evolution continues in each discipline of species though no defined statement has been published or researched to a singular origination. If similarities exist in the physical appearance then do comparisons exist in the mentality of all creatures? Off hand comparisons have been stated as in; 'a bad person has a bad dog' 'a sick person has a compassionate dog or cat' 'a child is protected by a vicious dog'. Just ask Ed. Though he associates with other humans he spends leisure time in observance of animals. It may just be a non scientific observation yet Ed has an opinion.

Old Pacos the light draft horse though big and assuming to be bold and destructive due to size is gentle and accepting of others invading its' space and attachment to its' body. When Ed cleans its' hooves, Pacos will lay its' head on Ed's shoulder with big lips tickling the nape of Ed's neck until laughter bursts from the man. A child of no conscious thought of danger can and has dashed beneath its' legs as if running an obstacle course around and between four legs and six inch diameter hooves. Pacos lowers its' head and watches with interest. Does a horse think and if so what does it think about?

What other similarities do creatures exhibit?

Who gives Ed the authority to judge any event that occurs in this world? In the forth coming narrative he is the only observer able to provide just the facts, no side commentary, no interpretations, no judgmental points of view, just the actual facts as they had occurred. Ed has a viewpoint to state on this matter and in his own words states;

'Details are of the most importance. What I observed had taken place where the incidents had occurred. I must not be judgmental, for that could cloud my testimony towards the perpetrators and even to the victims.

Motive is important to the victims and to those attained to judge and pass judgement to convict on behalf of the victims. Motive is only clear in the mind of the assailants. Sometimes that assailant never divulges that information prior to committing a crime nor through a trial nor after a conviction.

In this case, I only provide details of observation, no more, no less. When questioned, I must give just the facts. Detective Sergeant, Joe Friday made it simple and made a career of saying, 'Just the Facts, Sir.'

Just the Facts?

You, the reader may interpret, juggle the facts, make assumptions, and even pass judgement and condemn. What you cannot do is neither see what occurred, nor reverse, nor prevent what has happened.

Torture, rape and murder happened before my eyes. Why did I not intervene, prevent further escalations or inform proper authorities? Why? I am pondering these same questions and fail to arrive at a suitable answer.

In some ways I am a victim of circumstances and an accomplice to these events and will be judged by peers of society. Willingly I accept this, and say to you, the readers, that you may be my peers and judge me after you have digested all of the facts.

Spring weather had succumbed to the warmth of summer and lead into the beginning of a summer dry spell. Every person and every living animal, plant and insect was feeling the tension of a lingering parched season and idle time will create abstract thoughts and actions. All it takes is a location, idle time and bodies gathering. No need to identify neither by name nor by locale. It could be any location. No need to condemn this location that hosted the crime. By a green area surrounded by a linked fence, bodies gathered by a pond. Some strolled, others splashed and played in the cool water, and yet others congregated on the sidelines.

Groups, clicks, bands, tribes, gangs, call them what you will. We all partake in them in one form or another. Young mingle to play, middle age work in groups of co-workers just to be able to gather food for the family, and seniors gather to chat, complain about those of younger ages and snooze off at any moment. Then there are those adolescents, those attempting to enter, those of experience and those that should be mature enough to move on but stay on the fringes.

Off to one side by the fence, near the shade of overhanging trees that I first noticed the six individuals. They were a gang, a band, a clan. Call them what you will. These six hung together bonded by some abstract means. Three males and three females were paired up as observed by the way they huddled and fondled each other.

Of the six, two were of white completion. They were a couple. Though I noticed that they hung back, not flamboyant, not aggressive, yet they were a part of the group. It was the two other couples of black complexion expressing aggression, likely the leaders. It was obvious that the males were tight, one always backing the other. Those mouthy females always following their mates.

One male displayed domineering factors, big, aggressive and flamboyant in dress. His buddy, maybe not as big on structure was always in the thick of any shenanigans. That white fellow always at a distance yet within circle range and willing to assist verbally.

They were a group of concern. The whole community knew about them. Some turned a blind eye and a deft ear. Others squawked when out of hearing range. Even when innocent bystanders came under the group's harassment, no one expressed resentment nor offered condemnation. I am included among that lot of do nothing do-gooders.

Common bulling occurred over the early part of spring, it was expected by them and I witnessed the escalation. There was the some-what innocent splashing of water in the pond, chasing of the young ones out of the water, and dunking the young males not yet strong enough to fight back. Females just starting to mature into adolescence took a tongue lashing from the males. They taunted with sexual innuendoes. Then the female gang members would harass them, chase them and use a tone of voice that would humiliate and degrade.

That gang was on a mission, heading towards destruction. Blame it on breading, genetics, their heritage, their ancestors, society's environment, boredom or just the heat of the day or the fullness of an orange moon or by whatever means used to justify what this gang of hooligans did.

It is difficult to understand the randomness of whom they selected to pray upon. Does every creature have a designated path in life, pre destined? Why is it that some lead healthy lives, others sickly, some strong, others weak, smart, dumb, and yet some are singled out to be the victims in society? Why? I suppose there is a study going on somewhere. Earth and its inhabitants have been around an awful long time, yet answers to this dilemma have not come forth. From life's lottery, each draws a path to follow.

The Fowl Gang, a name for intended use because they flock together like birds of a feather and their tone of language is foul of mouth, had impressed on society their path in life. Into the surreal scene entered two immature females who had yet to draw a lottery ticket towards the path of life they were to take. Yet within days the first day toward an end would commence.

Like all youngsters, they want to emulate their peers, to be liked, to feel like a member of a click. Both females of the black complexion were watchful of the Fowl Gang. From a distance they watched, peeked so as not to be noticed, began walking, strutting, copying the gang's mannerisms. Little by little they ventured away from the open green area, away from the pond and beyond the verbal warnings of cautious elders.

Gang members noticed though paid little attention at first. As in every act of nature the Newbies ventured closer and hung around longer. Innocence was waning, they could not turn back.

Chatter from the white female instigated the initial taunting. Soon both black females played an innocent chase game. Run after the Newbies, chase them into the water then splash them. Laughter boldly sounded in all ears. Heads turned to watch. Not one single being attempted to interfere, to become involved, or act in a preventative measure. Eyes widened, heads swayed, then all returned to their previous status.

Yet again, unable, or reluctant to learn from the lessons from being harassed, both young females inched closer into the Fowl Gang's territory. After the Gang's females beckoned with voices and mannerisms of friendliness they rebuffed the Newbies. At this point two dark coloured males approached the Newbies, egged on by the circling white Gang member.

Playfully at first the males herded the females as if they were roaming cattle. Female Gang members voiced encouragement as if suggesting manhandling, to give them what they are asking for.

Who in their stable mind would want or expect to be manhandled, harassed and abused? In this instant the Gang had suggested and accepted the intent to manhandle. They closed in to press their bodies against, push, fondle and voice words of their intent. Where were the eyes, ears and voices of the community? Surely some had witnessed the incident in the early morning. Through the heavy haze of fog that drifted through the community, I had, yet I restrained myself to only viewing. I was studying the cause, effects and results of society, and would not interfere until the conclusion.

Like stock horse riders, the males separated the Newbies. With constant pushing and crowding they manoeuvred one female into a secluded area. Though not visible, the cries and sounds were vividly interpreted. They chased her, poking her, pushing, slapping, knocking her to the ground, fondling her, laying their bodies upon her, and performing the acts of intercourse. At a close distance the white male strutted, seemingly pleased with the actions of the two other males.

Beyond the locale where society carried on as if deft, dumb and blind, the female Gang members strutted about as if proud of what their mates were doing. What they were performing was torture. Why would a being want to inflict pain upon another? In a frenzy of adrenaline they scratched, slapped and bit the victim about the head, neck and vulnerable parts of the body.

What possible pleasure could be enjoyed by such an attack on an innocent being? Were they protecting their turf? Were the female Gang members feeling intimidated by the young Newbies, and executed an elimination order to their mates? Was it an initiation ritual inflicted before one could be accepted into the Gang? I offered myself these questions. By waiting to see the outcome then I could possibly obtain answers. I could not interject. I had to be only a witness. These events had to occur and play out to an end.

By late afternoon it had. Hours earlier the male Gang members strutted out three abreast bragging boastfully. Into the bosoms of their mates they were welcomed. All of society averted looking towards them. Eyes did focus on the young Newbie when she staggered towards home. Expressions were voiced, heads turned away but nothing was done to avenge what had been inflicted upon her. It is accurate to say that a percentage of the population would say that the female deserved what she got.

Battered is such a singular word, this female was stripped of her self worth, physically and mentally. Bare patches of skin showed about the head. Legs and arms lacked strength and coordination. Leaking from vacant eyes oozed blood and life shattering tears. No voice would ever be uttered from her bruised mouth. Mental rape was evident. Physical rape was possible, but torture both physically and mentally had taken its toll. Events seemingly subsided, though taunts from the Fowl Gang echoed whenever touring throughout the community.

Stripped of dignity by the Fowl Gang and by the community, the victim receded into a safe environment. Physically, her body was present. Her mind was no longer in the present reality. Confirmed to be blind and lacking strength for movement she sat alone near the green area of the park. Voices of the youth surrounded her, their innocent play soothing her tormented thoughts. Lack of nourishment deteriorated her strength. Lacking the will to eat, and for that matter the will to live.

Curled up in a fetal position on the lush grass she slept huddled among several toddlers. By late afternoon when her body grew cold the toddlers left to pursue their daily play. Society disposed of her body in the usual manner. I was commissioned with the task. Having witnessed the conclusion of this event, I was no closer to having concluding answers.

As is the progressiveness of crime, after one foray is committed, the criminal is excited and driven to accomplish a second. Not long after the Newbie perished, the Fowl Gang picked up where they had left off. Harassment of the second Newbie commenced. The pattern at first progressed in the same manner then incidents became bold, occurring within sight of all.

Unlike her friend, this Newbie was tougher, stood her ground and took the verbal abuse, the pushing and groping. As the incidents progressed she did not run, did not back down. In the minds of the Gang, they were being challenged and threatened. They enjoyed the chase, the adrenaline high obtained and the physical gratification. Being challenged hurt their image.

Pressured by the female Gang members and the white male, the aggravated black males having reached an excited pinnacle, pursued the young Newbie. Being in plain view of society and all others in the pond area of the green park the Gang members faced the young female.

Was it her fear or lack of fear that made her retain a stance? No female was going to intimidate those males. As cold as a slap to their faces they reacted. Both pinned the Newbie to the ground and pressed her face, neck and chest into the ground. Team work resisted her escape. While one held her down the other angrily raped for self gratification. Somewhat proud he stood over her extending chest and arms as if to say to the crowd, 'look at me, see my greatness.'.

In that moment of interlude, the female lurched free to stumble weakly away. Pouncing viciously the Gang leader again pinned her to the ground, his heavy body slamming her chest and neck into the dusty ground. Taking this advantage the second black male penetrated the female eagerly thrusting and squawking, imitating a frenzied dog gone mad.

Laying there in the billowing dust, her mouth and nostrils sucked in the choking particles. Beaten beyond recouping her dignity she lay there until a last exhaled breath shifted sand grains for the last time.

This is the truth as to what exactly happened. To swear to tell the truth in a court of law or to place a hand on the Holy Bible is the compulsory act that forces me to tell the truth. What will be hard to except by the readers of this story is to comprehend who the victims and criminals are.

Most of us believe that this sort of event may occur in a large Metro city, or on an off chance in a quaint town where nothing of this sort has ever happened. The victim usually is the sweet girl next door, the person most likely to succeed, the one chosen to be the Queen of the prom. Every criminal is the type cast gruesome fiend, to be from a poor background, uneducated and living on the streets.

Well, this case did not happen in a Metro city, nor in a small town, nor in a rural hamlet, it occurred in my back farm yard. The characters were Ducks! The Fowl Gang consisted of two female Rouen ducks, two male Rouen ducks, one male and one female Peaking ducks. The victims were immature Rouen ducks. The community consisted of a variety of Peaking and Rouen ducks and Embden geese.

The events happened as told. Questions I posted, unanswered. Conclusions and theories still left to be debated.

A trial was conducted by me sitting as judge and jury and I passed sentence. Upon the Fowl Gang they were sentenced to be executed as per guide-lines set out by the poultry and fowl farm act.

Internment of bodies in the deep freezer until discarded in the usual course of consumption.

No further criminal act has occurred here on the farm.

Food for thought.

A criminal duck tastes no different than an innocent duck. Both are delicious baked, roasted and stir-fried.'

Many will dismiss any comparisons between human behaviour and animal behaviour. Individually a person may use their sentient ability to agree or disagree. Ed will be the first to declare that he does not talk to animals and they do not talk back. This is not a fantasy as depicted in a movie. Whatever the relationship is between all creatures, it is what it is.

4

Fear has many applications and as many responses from people with a variable degree of reaction. Outwardly on a person's face there may be no indication of fear, yet inside, deep in thought the mind is reeling and the heart is fluttering. There are those that wear the extremes of fear with facial expressions and animated body gestures. It takes guts and inner strength to overcome fear. Then again a single occurrence will last a lifetime in the mind though the incident cannot be retrieved nor changed. What if previous actions could be relived, how would time from that moment be altered?

Though a particular encounter occurred fifty years earlier at the awkward adolescent year of sixteen, Ed still recalls the moment that weighed the balance of the future. Ed admits to himself that he did not have gumption, audacity to act upon emotions. The mind was the culprit, always judging on the side of caution.

The incident began with a girl having a liking for Ed and his Mother and Father informing the young lad that refusing the invitation was disrespectful. Father and Mother, in reminiscing of their youthful experiences, stated that the Sadie Hawkins dance was the one time of the year when the girl did the asking. For a shy person that was interested in life's experiences though did not have the ability to be forthright thought that it should be the girl that does all of the planning and asking. Ed would easily accept such an arrangement and would still be the man and always pay the tab. This changing of attitudes had not yet progressed in society so only once a year did the Sadie Hawkins dance provide a reversal of gender date asking.

Ed readily accepted without hesitation. If left to Ed those high school dances would be avoided or attended as a single. They were, except for this first Sadie Hawkins dance.

Being the oldest sibling there was no guidance from an older mentor and no guide book for an adolescent dummy. Ed should have taken pointers from the animal kingdom for there did not seem to be such humanistic problems in nature. When sitting, and observing life in general, the thoughts of this particular girl enters Ed's mind and questions form. Observing others is a way to see if an incident of fear is overcome or if the fear consumes a person.

Having grown up in the same neighbourhood and attended the same grade school they were comfortable as acquaintances. Girls do grow emotionally quicker than boys and seem to plan out life yet do not inform the boys they like. Ed seemed to be left in the dark. If asked, he would say that she was okay and that he liked her, but in grade school what more is he suppose to say or do? School mates said they were a couple and even Grandma liked her. She was tall, brownish blonde hair and nice looking and today Ed pictures her essence in the same memory. In a brief encounter in passing thirty years later, Ed saw the same girl, the same thin smile and upturned eyes that offered warmth. He should have called out after her and said hello.

While in thought during a rest period on a warm August day of haying, Ed watched a nephew being presented with a fear factor. Wiping sweat from brows, Father, Ed and younger brother Don rested while idle chatter focused on ways to stack square bails of hay. There is always a load of mass proportions to brag about. A year earlier a load had been stacked on the old wooden hay wagon that groaned with age. Three hundred bails though interlocked swayed top heavy while being pulled along the road. Only two bails had fallen off during the eighteen mile trek. Both had fallen within a mile of the barn's destination.

On this day only two hundred bails were stacked then unloaded at the barn. On the bails the men sat while twelve year-old T.J. swept loose hay off of the wagon bed. Tall, thin and well groomed T. J. did not seem suited to the farm–boy persona even though having lived next door to Uncle Ed's farm. Seeing the men resting, T.J. decided to sit on the wagon and dangle legs over the side. Although he did not work as hard as the men, it was warm out and a rest would suit him as well.

Absentmindedly listening to the men's conversation T.J.'s idle hands picked at hay strands and dropped them to the ground. Dry stems accumulated onto a useless pile to be devoured later by the horses and cows. Reaching out toward an object buried beneath loose hay, T.J. remarked in a questioning manner if anyone had lost a grey, green, yellow shoelace?

Each man having heard T.J.'s question eyed their footwear. Don slightly lifted eyes over knees while leaning comfortably back against a bail of stacked hay. Kicking out a leg, Father glanced at leather footwear. Having his chin resting on a hand of an arm resting on a knee, Ed peeked down at dust colouring coating black boots. Their western style boots lacked the need to be laced.

A treasure found mingled in among loose hay usually happens though value and condition may be worse than perfect. Ed had found an antler from a deer, a can of unknown contents, a skeleton of a bird and odd bones of various varmints. A multi coloured shoelace was T.J.'s first find.

Picking up the shoelace was a natural act. The feel and texture expected of a fabric or even a leather shoelace was not consistent. A slight mushy feel as would be expected of a wet, worn shoelace hung draped over T.J.'s clean callous free fingers.

It was when the shoelace moved and wiggled between finger grip that T.J. noticed one fat end and a tapered other end. A screech sound out of the mouth of the young boy brought heads of the men to lift. Eyes witnessed T.J. bounce from the wagon and a hand dropping the shoelace. Instantly the hand was wiped repeatedly against a pant leg.

When the heavy end of the shoelace moved and eyes blinked in the small head is when T.J. muttered in a stuttering explanation that the grey, green, yellow shoelace was a snake. Bewildered stares from the men met T.J.'s wide frightened eyes. The men leaned forward to peek down on the small creature lying with its' yellow belly upward.

Slowly the small innocent garter snake twisted and curled to roll onto its' stomach. Surely it was dazed and confused in these new surroundings. At one moment it had been slithering across a field then raked in among hay, pressed and bound within a hay bail. Trapped, it endured bouncing, stacking and a long rocking ride then shaken loose at Ed's farm.

Little eyes blinked and a split tongue taste tested its' surrounding. From a distance T.J. watched over the men's shoulders. Ed, Father and Don leaned forward to watch the snake's next move. Satisfied that the large creatures were not going to grab or stomp upon it, the tiny fellow slithered slowly toward the side of the barn. 'This would be as good a home as anyplace,' suggested Father knowing that it would be useless to return the snake to its' original home. Hay fields were vast and varied in locations making it difficult to pin-point the snake's original location.

Did the little encounter affect T.J.? Did this little grey, green, yellow garter snake instil fear in the future makeup of T.J.? If fear is not conquered or controlled then a different path in life may be taken. At an age when children mature and venture from the nest, T.J. moved to the city and a career that is as far and different than the rural life and the inhabitants of nature.

Did Ed's fear alter his future situation and result in his bachelor status? Willingly he accepted the girl's invitation to the dance. This awkward first date was documented by a picture that Mother insisted on taking of the couple before the events unfolded throughout the evening. Ed's date paid for the dance, asked for selected dances, held his hand and proposed the mock wedding and applied a slight kiss after pronounced wed by the Sadie Hawkins preacher.

This was all easy, for Ed did not have to do the asking or planning. Shyness could be side stepped. What to do after the Sadie Hawkins dance? The mind would be thinking negatively and enhance the shyness and the implications of rejection. Then there was the walk home and escorting of the girl to her home after midnight. The privileges of the Sadie Hawkins day was over and Ed would now have to make decisions and . . . yes, make a move, give her a kiss goodnight. Time seemed to last forever and at the same time slowed down on the walk down darkened streets. All Ed could think of was how would he kiss her, what words needed to be spoken, or should he just lean in with eyes closed and accept what happens? What if nothing happens? What if eyes are opened and she is gone. Even worse would be her laughing and mocking Ed with a humorous grin.

They had reached her home and lingered with small talk in the shadow of the porch light. Time stood still yet the arms of time passed twelve-fifteen, twelve-thirty, twelve-forty-five and still Ed plotted an approach to a kiss though physically stood stiffly back.

He had to make a move before her parents turned on more internal lights or heaven forbid opened the door to confront the couple. Ed decided to make a move, now, no in a second, when she looks up, no, when her head is turned he would cup her face then lean in, no, he should ask if he could kiss her?

Out of nowhere a voice breaks the couple's concentration when her older brother arrives home from the dance. All he said was, 'hurry up and kiss her,' before entering the house and closing the porch light. Though the closing of the light was a nice understanding gesture, his words interrupted the mood and Ed's conflict between shyness and desire.

No kiss bonded a possible companionship despite others saying they were meant to be together; they did not become a couple. At moments of reflection Ed wonders what their lives would have been like had he kissed her. Even now in his sixties, which is the new forties, shyness and the conflict between do it and do not do it is still playing out in his mid.

What if the kiss had occurred?

5

All creatures communicate among themselves and between species. Vocal communication is the most common; just listen to ravens and their multiple calls. There is a caw sound emitted over distance to indicate location of others. A guttural throat sound to indicate the finding of a food source. Then the squawking, squeaking sounds between resident and vagrant ravens arguing and insulting each other over matters of importance or just for the sake of creating controversy.

At any given encounter Ed will participate in raven banter. It is likely that Ed does not know the meaning of each call and may use it at inappropriate times. Being pissed off, a raven may curse Ed with a vocal slur before flying off to inform others of the crazy human.

Humans are able to verbally state their emotions toward animals and offer compassion, scorn, sympathy, praise and condemnation. It is questionable to the amount of understanding the animal is able to comprehend? In turn are animals able to provide their versions toward humans.

Buttermilk, a female Appaloosa, would stare at Ed when commands were stated. Often Ed thought the mare was playing dumb. Registration papers proved its' lineage though from the visual study the horse did not resemble the Appaloosa breed. Buttermilk as the name suggests is a creamy milk colour with only one black spot on the rump.

The lineage of the Appaloosa breed did not apply to Buttermilk. Appaloosa horses are praised as sturdy plains and trail horses with a temperament of easy compatibility, companionship and sure footing. Companionship and ease of handling described Buttermilk. Adventurous the horse was not. Open the gate to the field fine and Buttermilk would willingly go. Open the gate at night to bed down and feed, no problem, Buttermilk was first in. Hint at opening a gate to the freedom of the wild to travel trails and open country for exploration, and stuck in the corner the mare would stay, refusing to venture out. Always the mother figure of the herd the mare would continuously neigh, calling to others until all arrived back home.

Trail riding with Pacos, the large gelding, was just two pals out exploring. Nothing seemed to disturb the Clydesdale-Palomino-Hackney cross breed. With firm bulk the gelding walked and trotted with a smooth stride, a delight for the rider, no jarring or bouncing. A draw back was that Pacos constantly ate, always munching on branches and peeling off leaves. The sweet moist leaves complimented the seed heads of tall grass. So complacent the old boy was, often Pacos did not pay attention of direction, obstacles or critters.

Though Ed assumed that Pacos did not pay attention the opposite is true. Between nibbles and with a mouthful of trailside leaves, Pacos stopped, quite munching and flared nostrils and snorted. 'Always trust the instincts of an animal,' Ed reminded himself in thought. Sitting comfortable in the saddle, Ed waited and watched Pacos' head point in a direction then seemingly follow the movement of a scent.

Ed sniffed the air and drew in hints of sweet pollen, fresh leaf smells and varied bark scents of birch, maple, oak and alder trees then a distinctive wet wool blanket smell. Pacos' head turned from one side of the trail to the other. Satisfied that the smell had ventured into the bush Pacos lowered its' head, relaxed acoustic catching ears, snorted out excess scent molecules from nostrils then commenced munching.

On its' own initiative Pacos continued walking on while Ed's head rotated and bobbed while eyes tried to see through the bush. Glancing to the trail; Ed's eyes widened at the sight of bear paw prints freshly imprinted in the moist soil of the bush trail. Stiffening in the saddle, Ed's legs pressed against Pacos' ribs in an indication of an instruction to move. Pacos paid no heed though turned its' head to send a questioning stare at Ed. Obviously the glare stated, 'do not worry, the bear is moving on and minding its' own business, I am not worried.'

Ed was worried and lightly back kicked boot heels into Pacos' belly. This did not work and would not work with a second or third kick. At a leisurely pace Pacos ambled on with more concern focused on reaching for the next branch of leafy substance. The pull and snap-back of the branch slapped Ed comically in the face. Did Pacos purposely do it and then silently snicker?

Whether or not an animal visually displays awareness, animals are as Pacos proved with the crossing of the bear. On following encounters when Ed assumed that Pacos was more concerned with food and not watching where big feet stepped, Ed's fears were unfounded.

At a rise in the trail at the Gros Cap Bluffs the trail is a ledge cascading down a cliff to Lake Superior's Cambrian shield shore. Brother Marc riding Tceque, an Arabian-Quarter horse cross breed, lead the way and navigated the thin ledge. Pacos' girth is twice that of

Tceque and surely would be brushing Ed's leg against the rock wall. As usual Pacos seemed to be dreaming in la-la land when stepping on the slippery surface of rock of the ledge. Without rhyme or apparent reason Pacos decided to turn around on a ledge edge cascading into free falling air-space.

Deftly large feet turned until its' large body rotated into the opposite direction and lips pulled a small blueberry bush from a crevice. Satisfied to fill its' mouth Pacos turned again. The clip-clip of steel shoes on rock sent tinny pebbles tinkling over the edge. Without concern for Ed's safety or its' own, Pacos seemed fully relaxed with this manoeuvre. Happily satisfied with a mouthful of feed to chew on, Pacos followed the black swishing tail of Tceque.

Safely down from the high trail and on the flats of the marsh, Tceque suddenly side stepped the trail. Hooves danced and its' head turned and snorted with discuss at the avoided object on the trail. Arabian breeds are a bid skittish and seem to be hot blooded and a complete opposite of Pacos' attitude. The old gelding's big feet enhanced to look larger by the long hock hair gingerly stepped cautiously over a garter snake crossing the trail. Ed glanced down anticipating seeing back hooves pressing the reptile into the mud. A hoof hovered above then the leg muscles drew forward and planted the foot clear of the snake.

Pacos knew what it was doing on the trail, on the cliff ledge and when walking over the snake. Ed has observed from the beginning to let Pacos do what he does and not to try and force changes by heel directions or pulling on the reins. Animals in a way train humans.

There is unspoken communication ability between Pacos and Ed. A means of knowing what the other wants without the need to grunt, neigh, pull a rein, shake head or plough a hoof at the ground. All of this invisible ability to communicate is thrown out with the garbage when food is concerned. When seeing or smelling any hint of food its' nostrils flare, ears perk, eyes widen and Pacos struts with a royal gait towards a meal. Not a mundane animal feed meal, rather the aroma of human food fare.

A first instant was a sneak attack. Ed had been leaning on a fence rail chatting to a neighbour and eating a beef sandwich. Sneaking along the fence with wide inquisitive eyes, Pacos inched closer and extended lips to lap at the edges of the free meal. The dexterity of lips and tongue in co-operative coordination is miraculous. Bread, lettuce, cucumber and the mustard-ketchup condiment was striped away leaving Ed's fingers holding the unwanted beef.

Horse lips smacked as Pacos' big head searched Ed's hands, neck, pockets and behind ears for further delicacies. This was the beginning of a continuous assault by Pacos upon Ed whenever food was concerned. Ed could not eat in front of Pacos, could not rein tie the old boy to the fence and eat at a distance when observing big brown eyes pleading for a nibble.

Once down from the bluffs and on the rocky shore to take in the lustre of white capped waves splashing against rocks it was time to eat. One small bite for Ed is a corner of the sandwich, one small bite for Pacos is half of the sandwich. Having previous experience with peanut butter and jelly sandwiches the old gelding was adept with the ability to separate the bread and jelly from the peanut butter. On the tongue and roof of the mouth the bread and jelly teased taste buds before swallowed. Preventing peanut butter from sticking to the roof of the mouth Pacos diverted the sticky substance to stay between lips and outer gums to be savoured over time.

While Pacos spent time savouring the lasting stickiness, Ed managed to devour his share of lunch. Brother Marc faired better in successfully eating an entire lunch. Tceque, the polite, well mannered Arabian-Quarter horse cross did not like peanut butter and jelly sandwiches and refrained from bothering Marc.

As different as the variables of humans, animals have their own peculiarities. Unlike Pacos who is forthright and pleasantly aggressive with invading Ed's presence, Buttermilk, the cream coloured Appaloosa is a well mannered mother figure of the group. The mare will politely wait until the menagerie of horses, cows and goats tangle for mouthfuls of offered food bits. Standing behind the foray the old girl will patiently wait until Ed approaches and offers an individual share. Waiting means not having to fight between every animal's lips vying for a morsel. A loving pat and scratch between ears is a bonus.

All females regardless of species have stubbornness. This is an observation point of view Ed has documented. Buttermilk has stubbornness and a motherly concern over the other horses and even all of the various farm residents. On a riding training excursion the motherly mare proved to be stubborn and also expressed concern for the well being of Ed.

Unwilling to leave the security of the farm the mare worries when others leave and calls after them. With affection the old girl will greet returning horses with head and neck rubbing. No horse paid attention or worried when Ed brought the mare out past the farm gate for the trail riding training.

Though accepting Ed's directions to walk on, Buttermilk's ears faced backwards and eyes strained to view the farm fading from sight. Frogs croaking and birds chirping made the horse nervous, skittish and frightened to be away from the security of home. Miles from home Buttermilk still neighed, pleading a request for fellow horses to respond. Lack of response caused the mare to whinny as if pleading for Ed to return to the sanctuary of tall grass fields boarded by fence rails.

Stepping gently along a dry mud trail close to the shores of the St. Marys River the horse lowered head and ears to duck beneath low branches. Pacos would be stripping the branches of foliage. Buttermilk worried more about unknown creatures ahead on the trail.

In a low area the dry mud began to soften from water of a shallow creek. Summer dryness had reduced the creek to a shallow six inch deep, three foot wide puddle of frog utopia. Ed had paid little attention to Buttermilk's lowered head and turned ears. Maybe the walk and nervousness made the horse thirsty. Not the case! In an instant where time seems to create a void between the present and the future Buttermilk bucked. A single rump motion of back legs springing upward and front legs planted firmly rocketed Ed out of the saddle.

A perfect flip a circus tumbling performer could not have executed any more perfect than Ed's forward flip. The landing a unique flat position on his back with head inches away from the water's edge. Nothing other than blue sky before Ed's eyes and a shadow of Buttermilk's head leaning over the creek. Concerned eyes seemed to ask if Ed was okay. The landing was smooth on cushioning forest moss and dry. A bonus was not landing in the creek.

Doing a mental check Ed waited for indications of pain before beginning to move fingers, toes, legs and arms. Satisfied that there were no injuries Ed rolls over and stands facing Buttermilk. Seeing that its' rider is okay, Buttermilk slowly turns to begin walking back along the trail then stops at the opening of a clearing and waits.

The first thoughts in Ed's mind is that of Buttermilk not wanting to get hooves wet, thus the reason for the abrupt ejection. Stepping easily across the creek, Ed called for Buttermilk to stand. Which she did until Ed arrived at a point of ten feet away before continuing back along the trail and homeward bound. At the crossing of trail and road the mare stopped waited and looked back to see if Ed was following.

Knowing the conditions of the world environment the old girl turned its' head in both directions before crossing the road safely. At a distance Buttermilk stopped and turned a stare to watch Ed cross the road safely. Satisfied that this situation was under control, repeated horse actions continued throughout the mile walk home.

Buttermilk was truly concerned for the safety of Ed, though the mare needed to hurry home to the security of the farm and comfort of home. With head bowed and pointed at the latch of the gate big brown eyes watched Ed slowly advancing. Ed's facial expression was of anger, eyes bewildered and thoughts surprised that Buttermilk had returned to the farm only when satisfied that he had followed. Ed opened the gate, leaned with both arms on the top rail and with a foot up on the lower rail.

Guilty ears tuned forward and down, one eye slightly turned toward the man in anticipation of a command. Ed hesitated. Buttermilk stood stiffly tentative. Not until Ed's soft voice stated, 'Go on, walk in,' did Buttermilk enter. There is a conflict in this matter, whether to punish Buttermilk with more training for leaving or offer food as praise for not running off wild and returning home?

Ed mounted and put the mare through walking, trotting and backing manoeuvres before giving a brush down and food. The old girl trailed behind Ed as he headed for the gate and it gave a neighing comment. Not understanding horse talk, Ed assumed the nasal neigh to be an apology, or a possible sarcastic 'na-na-na'.

6

Eggs had been in the incubator for the required twenty-eight days and Ed eagerly anticipated the first hatching of poultry chicks. Every year is the same, yet every year it is a wonderment of expectations to see tiny beaks pecking through the dry shells. In the same way parents wonder if their child will be male or female and have the required amount of toes and fingers, Ed speculated on the hatchlings being hens or roosters. A bonus is to see the varieties of colours of down coverings.

Ed is not a particular man in the same way that selective breeders are. The purity of individual breeds and a specific lineage does not play an important roll when free breading on Ed's farm. All breeds of chickens intermingle and mate resulting in a variety of colours, sizes and shapes of plumage. Along with the visual aspect arrive multiple personalities.

As is the case in human evolution, disabilities and handicaps happen in poultry breading. Unlike Hop-along who suffered a hindrance from an external cause, newborn chicks may suffer deformations, coordination problems, blindness, deftness and even nakedness due to too many or not enough or improper mixing of the gentle stuff that defines a normal chicken.

Ed is not up on the intricacies of evolutionary science or knows the reasons why, and why not, yet visually sees the results in newly born chicks. Every year a percentage do not make it past a day or a week. Only the fit survive. Mental problems do not seem as prevalent in early deaths. Physically they grow healthy and only begin to display the quirks when older. The gambit unfolds from constant pecking; shaking of head, shyness, bullying, walking backwards and the need to run for no apparent reason.

An average sized egg had a small pin hole in the shell on an inspection in the morning. Ed speculated that the first chick of the season would break through by late in the evening. Having the first indication of hatching, Ed checked in every hour as a nervous expectant father would.

At a noon hour check Ed witnessed a large chick bursting from the egg as if the chick was cramped into an inadequate small space. All seemed normal; the shell fell away when legs kicked free and wings stretched. Obviously tired from the strain of escaping the tight casing the whitish-yellow chick rested. Under the warmth of the incubator heating coil wet fuzz dried and fluffed. Lunch would be delayed while Ed waited for the chick to discard the rest of the shell covering half of the head, neck and back.

When the chick managed to roll onto legs and feet and balance, Ed knew something was wrong. The shell should have fallen off easily. A thin moist pliable membrane should be between the shell and chick. If the shell is not discarded easily then heat from the incubator will fuse the shell to skin and down and result in problems.

Picking up the chick, Ed inspected the attached shell. It was dry. Gently crumbling the shell with fingers he removed pieces a little at a time in an attempt to reduce stress on the new born chick. Not until the last piece covering one side of the face that the condition of a deformity was viewed. The top of the skull on one side was indented; the left eye sealed shut and the top beak twisted to the right over the bottom beak twisted to the right.

Though the chick was lively in his hands, Ed expressed disappointment in the fact that the first chick of the season may not make it past the day let alone a week. By chance if physical ability extended life, would the indentation of the skull deformation against the brain cause mental disabilities?

Humans have the ability to think abstractly in ways of studying themselves and in researching ancestors. Why, in order to understand where features originate; mannerisms, intelligence, physical stamina and each minor intelligence a person displays. Knowing of his own early learning problems and how he needed to find ways to learn, Ed wondered if the defect was handed down genetically.

In a time when the three R's were being taught, teachers had a mandate to teach and expected students to comply. There was no understanding when a student struggled with comprehension. Poor grade marks were applied and accompanied by comments in a negative form; 'the student does not strive to learn' 'student day dreams' 'student is introverted and does not participate'.

Learning disabilities were not studied. Corrective measures were unheard of. Those with learning problems were discounted, left behind, given a failing grade, placed in the slow learner's class. Many were left behind and future lives reflected in their life styles and types of jobs obtained and their status in society. In hindsight, Ed has made the connection when observing known persons. At the young age of five when entering the educational system he did not have the ability to predict the future. Yet, he knew that his learning ability was different than the other children.

At that first introduction into the mystery of education a hidden brain function decided that an alternate way of learning is required. This brain function operated without Ed's conscious thought and would serve him throughout life. At the age of sixty, Ed still uses tricks devised throughout the educational years to tackle current problems.

Speaking and understanding only French at five years old was a setback when dropped off by Father into an English school. Father spoke in a foreign language to a nun in the echoing hall of a building then spoke French to Ed. Father indicated to Ed that he was bringing him to a place where many children would be playing. Again speaking a foreign language to a woman he withdrew a hand from Ed's tight grip. This first meeting of similar shaped and aged children did not unfold as expected. The children earnestly greeted Ed with voices of mumble jumble un-interpretive sounds. A blank bewildered face with eyes wide questioned their babbling. Losing interest, the children returned to small chairs circling a larger chair. Despite the motherly looking woman indicating for Ed to join the rest and take a seat, Ed stood stiffly with thoughts of escaping the room's confines.

This was the first incident of neglect. The teacher and uninterested students forgot about the boy defiantly standing at the door. Eyes of a blonde haired girl seemed fixated on the new boy and continued to point to an empty chair next to her. 'Sitting beats standing,' must have been a concluding thought for Ed for he took a seat.

Being a French speaking child was a learning handicap among English speaking people. Through osmosis of continuous input of English words and imitative responses Ed learned English throughout that first year of school. His mind must have locked the vault in the part of the brain that computes the French language. No longer would he speak the French language and to this day is unable to speak nor think in the French language.

Though parents, grandparents and relatives on both sides of the family speak French, Ed refused to participate. Subconsciously his mind translated the intake of French words into English and the converted family stories are still retained in his memory to this day.

Dyslexia was not a known word to a child, let alone the meaning. In his forties Ed began to put the pieces together and reflect on the difficulties of learning during those grade school years. When all other children were drawing flat representations of their homes, Ed drew a three dimensional representation. Yet this was not impressive to the teachers, it was the backward placements of letters of Edmond's name that the teacher harped upon.

Forward or backward positions of letters or numbers was not a big deal for Ed, he knew what they were. A first trick developed by Ed was to print the letters real small on the guidelines of the paper then pretend to look in a mirror and print the letters larger in reverse. It worked. Reading became a challenge, yet over time speed of the mind increased with the ability to reverse the letters. With age, especially the later years of his fifties Ed finds himself hesitating when reading and a need to think about a letter's correct position is pondered.

It was not Ed that had a problem, it was everyone else. If the letters were left the way Ed saw them then there would not be a problem. This was just the natural way his mind perceived the written word. Why were others forcing him to change?

Ed did not worry about the problems encountered as a child; it just took a bit of thinking to solve the problem and find tricks to help. This he also did with math and the use of numbers. Dyslexia encompasses a scale of impairment and associated difficulties. Some people with dyslexia see complete words in sentences all mixed up or floating and moving. Memory and recollection is more of an inconvenience for Ed. Recalling or memorizing dates, telephone numbers, street addresses and important time frames is a drastically lacking ability. Ed does know his own birth date, telephone number, street address and the telephone numbers of two brothers. This is the limitations. A sister's number must be looked up, for she lives out of town. Personal names of people must be repeated and recalled constantly in order to be memorized.

Name recall can be embarrassing at times, though Ed holds no importance to dates and telephone numbers. Einstein once implied that there is no reason for cluttering the brain with trivial data providing that a person knows how to retrieve information from a book of recorded information.

Some people with dyslexia develop other abilities to compensate for difficulties. A photo graphic memory reduces the need to read. Some may be strong willed and are able to designate others to do the required work to solve a problem. Unfortunately Ed does not have those abilities. What Ed does have is the ability to recall stories, incidents, details, people's faces and their mannerisms, likes, dislikes and recalls events of previous meetings and conversations.

Ed's stories will be void of specific clock times, year, day, month, a person's name and any location number or contact information. What will surprise people will be the unfolding story of what may have transpired and the details of a person's actions, emotions and accurate dialogue.

Math was a different matter. Remember that Ed's schooling was before the new teaching methods of math, before metric, before calculators and computers. To this day Math computing within the mind is useless. All calculations must be accomplished on paper.

Seeing fellow students counting on fingers on one hand then the other and even fingers on hands of neighbouring students, Ed laughed slightly within. Not that Ed felt superior; it was the visual actions of students using fingers with less than useful quality. Ed never dared to display his inability to do math by enhanced animation. Still, math had to be accomplished. Over time Ed devised a method of an infinite dot system on a see-through cube. Add, subtract, multiply and divide as fast as a person can do a calculation in their mind and on fingers and toes, Ed accomplished with dots on a paper.

Ed does use a calculator now; though at times will double check with his dot system. The system was not self created and Ed will admit this. The basic idea of dots entered his thoughts on a visit to meet a cousin of the same age. Ed and Marc were between six and seven years of age when Ed first adapted a dot system. Marc had been ninety percent blind since birth. His vision limited to shadows. This did not stop the pair from being rambunctious children in their exploration of life.

What did impress Ed was how Marc could cheat legally in school. Marc was able to read brail by dragging fingers over little dots on paper. Then he did math by feeling dots representing numbers. This is where Ed adapted brail dots to his see-through cube. Any number of dots could be added, subtracted, multiplied or divided by penciling dots on each surface of the cube.

Easily frustration could have prevented Ed from progressing. Learning disabilities have hindered many young students in the past. Learning and teaching has progressed, too late for some. Ed, for whatever reason or desire used creative methods to adapt and succeed.

The question of genetics does interest Ed. Did the absent gene that is anointed to be dyslexia come from parents, their parents and so forth back generations? Could it be the odds plus or minus that is given to each person by the luck of the draw or spin of the roulette wheel? Studying ancestors and their IQ's may give Ed a comparison.

IQ's are not a true indication of intelligence or ability. Each person is intelligent and skilful in their own selective areas.

In tracing family linage, Ed researched as far back as possible, picking his father's side first in order to find out about each person's abilities or lack of.

During the era of the expansion towards the west and tales of open plains and endless herds of Bison, Ed's great-great-grandfather considered the lore. This was the mid eighteen-hundreds when the dignified east was civilized and towns were becoming socialized cities. The west came to life in newspaper articles glorifying the native wars in the United States, their civil war and the cowboy life enhanced with outlaws and lawmen settling differences with gun-fire. In Canada with less drama unfolded the Reil conflict and the glory of prestige of the North-West mounted Police always apprehending their man without gun-fire. Canada has a history as exuberant and variable as their neighbouring country of the United States, though Canadians are humble they often do not brag and exploit with bravado.

Great-great-grandfather Thomas studied world events in an educational system yet wished to live the life of adventures. Not born into privilege, though the family's status in the community allowed for the formal education of Thomas. With applied tendencies Thomas achieved the distinguished level of a College-University scholar. This achievement in education did not sustain success in fortunes or prestige in future years.

Seeking adventure, Thomas set forth from Quebec and only reached the middle of Ontario on a westward journey. Homesteading in the Massey area of Ontario he and wife Julia settled down to raise six daughters and one son. Julia, of French and Native Canadian blood, having educational skills home schooled their children.

Thomas and Julia did not achieve success that is assumed to arrive with education. They did have success in a long marriage and children and grandchildren. Their homestead sustained life though lacked worth. In the current era of twenty-fourteen the location of the farm land is the remnants of a sand pit.

Ed concluded that great-great-grandparents were educated people with intelligence though may have lacked manual skills to accompany the mental abilities.

Bartheleme, great-grandfather of Ed and an only son seemed unconcerned with the need for a formal education. As a son he was expected to work on the farm which he did while attempting other occupations in life. When age of maturity arrived he ventured towards the pleasures of life which included the female variety. Producing children to populate Canada at the turn of the century seemed to be his talent. Education and physical trades were not pursued. Common today is to be unmarried and raise children. This was frowned upon in the late eighteen-nineties and early nineteen-hundred.

Out of wedlock arrived a child to be considered part of the family though raised by the mother's parents. Undaunted by the situation Bartheleme and Delila continued a courtship and eventually married and raised fourteen children. Unlike Thomas who lived into his eighties, Bartheleme died in his forties. As rumour goes, he passed away at the dining table, his head resting to sleep in a plate of mashed potatoes. Great-grandmother's skills lay in the care and rearing of a brood of children.

Education seemed to be unimportant and somewhat left up to the children to accept or not to pursue. Though available in the years between nineteen-four and nineteen-twenty, Grand-father Edmond decided that physical work was more important an education than formal schooling. Could it be that Edmond had a learning disability? He could not read or write. This factor did not stop him from learning and advancing in the trade of carpentry, specifically in timber construction in the mines of Northern Ontario. Grand-mother Yvonne took care of the reading and writing aspects and transcribing mathematical calculations for grand-father. Numbers and math was not a problem for grand-father. It was the lack of ability to write down calculations. Using a carpenter square, Grand-father was able to make calculations in a way that a side rule does. So, lacking reading and writing abilities, he excelled in physical trades and mental math.

When father arrived in the late nineteen-twenties the great depression and the dirty thirties affected the livelihood of families. The educational system had expanded and began to demand attendance for the grade school years or to the age of twelve. Father, Fern, had attended until the sixth grade where after that point a need to help the family meant working. Despite only reaching the sixth grade, Father was able to read and write in French and English and speak both languages. He may not have been a scholar, yet contained self intelligence to accomplish working tasks.

Mother, Georgette, managed to reach the eighth grade before venturing into the working years of a young woman. Equal to Father, Mother also was able to read and write French and English and speak both languages. The ability to accomplish mathematical calculations in her mind often astonished Ed. Mother did not need a slide rule, pen and paper nor a calculator in her elder years.

Ed was often amazed with Mother's ability when accompanying her at a grocery store. Knowing that she only had a fixed amount of money in her possession she would select items, add, subtract, multiply and divide calculations in her mind. Items would be placed in the shopping cart, removed from the cart and replaced by other items and at all times the price calculations would be computed. When checking out at the cashier counter the items equalled the funds available, maybe slightly under but never, never over.

Ed pondered his lack of abilities accounted for by dyslexia, the abilities to adapt and abilities in trades to that of his ancestors. Great-great-grandparents were fairly well educated; great-grandfather not so much, great-grandmother minimal education. Grandfather had no formal education though excelled in trades. Grandmother had suitable education offered for the times. Father had suitable education and functional labour skills. Mother also had suitable education and excellent math skills.

There were similarities in Ed's make-up to that of his ancestors though only comparisons. Without testing and physical contact there is no way to make a concrete conclusion. Stories are passed down though content can be vague. Great-great-grandfather graduated from college, Ed graduated from college. Grandfather may have been dyslexic and unable to read of write. Ed has dyslexic learning disabilities. Grandfather was a carpenter; Ed is a carpenter. Father was a physical working man; Ed is a physical working man.

Great-grandfather left little of a history due to the fact that he died fairly young. Maybe great-grandfather was a story teller and this is the similarity in common with Ed, who excels in story telling and cowboy poetry recitations.

Though Ed has tried to find a link to his ancestors to reflect on his essence of body and mind it has still been illusive. Each ancestor is a mixture of previous ancestors, a mixture of adding ingredients randomly selected to form the next descendent and Ed is one result.

Eyeing the chick with visual deformity, Ed acknowledged that it was the result of chance. Colour, size and shape are a part of genetics and the deformity a result of incubation conditions. Big Bertha, a name Ed anointed the chick, would have to overcome its' disability in order to survive. Ed held little hope though wished for its' survival to beat the odds.

Among the hatchlings to follow, Bertha seemed less intelligent and acted strangely. It did not sleep, walk or peck in the way the others did. Bertha swayed from side to side; slept on its' back, walked in constant clockwise direction towards the side of the sealed eye and indented skull. It would peck then lift its' head and shake then repeat the actions. Despite this Bertha was surviving and growing at a faster rate than the other chicks. Bertha was a hen in the shape and size of a growing rooster.

By six weeks Bertha ruled the roost over hens and roosters. Of all the hatchlings that spring, Bertha was the only one that would greet and walk toward Ed when he entered the yard or hen house. Only Bertha accepted feed from his open palm. Could it be the slight assistance Ed applied when it struggled in early life? Ed would roll the sleeping chick onto feet and assist it to walk until it gained balance and found food offered in hand. Had this gesture bonded chick and man?

Even at full growth Bertha did not roost, it slept in a hen cube nest on its' left side with head tucked under the right wing. When walking in a constant clockwise direction every third step would be slightly off balance as the head shook. Other chickens were a bit upset at feeding time around the circular feeder when Bertha would peck and continuously circle. Each chicken would squawk and back allowing Bertha to pass. Not one chicken, hen or rooster resented or picked on Bertha despite its' oddity and constant annoying ways.

When watching with interest Ed wondered if all consciously understood Bertha's disabilities and made allowances.

Bertha stood out among the chickens; comically, friendly, large and stately in feathers of white among reddish brown kin. A chicken is a chicken and on the farm a hen is required to lay eggs. If a chicken is not an egg layer then it is a meat bird. Not one egg was ever laid by

Bertha, yet Ed let it be to live to old age. A sigh of sadness Ed did express through a day of mourning when Big Bertha passed on one warm summer morning. Sleep just takes a chicken when it reaches old age. Ed misses the old chicken that struggled to survive. Despite disabilities it did enjoy its' days on the farm.

7

Every once in a while there is a need for a change in the flow of daily life. For whatever reason, Ed attended a play production at a small theatre. Maybe it was the performance that enticed him to question his ability to perform and possibility of joining the amateur theatre group. Being a writer, Ed looked at this venture as an extension, a means of developing the performance aspect of the written word.

A simple inquiry instantly resulted in an invitation to attend informative workshops, readings and open cast calls for a next production by the Sparks Theatre Group. With anxiety, based on the fact that Ed is not outgoing and shyness prevents openness in groups, accepted a small part requiring the recitation of a prose segment. One prose segment of ten lines seemed workable and this was accepted. This small introduction would provide confidence and pressure Ed to be more outgoing within groups. Well it did not. Though the recitation and ease of acting unfolded without frustration, Ed's social interacting did not change. Shyness and the standing outside of the mix still prevailed.

What arrived next, when Ed was comfortable with inclusion in the theatre group and providing a small contribution to the forthcoming play, was a request by the director. Shyness and a lack of courage to say no, Ed found him-self accepting a larger part and five more prose sections to recite. Someone had bowed out of the production leaving a spot to be filled . . . apparently by Ed.

'So be it,' was Ed's reaction. Dyslexia played a hindrance in a form of a need for Ed to read over and over and over in order to memorize the prose. Constant recitation during the day, evening, during meals, during farm chores and any spare moment was required to overcome the memory hindrance of dyslexia. This recitation occurred relentlessly over the two months prior to the first evening presentation.

During a lull on a warm afternoon of carrying out farm chores, Ed took a moment to sit on a top rail of the fence and recite to a farm animal audience. Horses, cows and goats munched lazily or grabbed sleep time by stretching out under the warm sun. Only Cheyenne, a tall light toned coloured horse, approached Ed sitting on the fence and rested a large head on the man's legs. It did seem as if the mare listened with interest.

Cheyenne and Sierra are sisters a year apart in age and the daughters of Sanorra, the sister of Pacos. The ancestry linage was passed down and both horses exhibited the features of the Clydesdale-Palomino-Hackney breeds. Pacos displayed the golden colour of the Palomino in the summer then the change of colour to pure white long hairs of the Hackney horse during the winter months. Bushy hock hair and large hooves expressed the Clydesdale features. Sister Sanorra retained the bright colouring of golden year round. Sierra, the elder daughter was completely white with blue-white eyes, almost an albino rating. The mare had the size and physical structure of Sanorra and Pacos. Horse temperament was equal to that of her mother, stubborn and semi friendly.

Cheyenne was an opposite and more social like that of Pacos, her uncle. Tones of light brown, beige, white and reddish brown varied in balanced patterns over the body. Unlike a very docile temperament of Pacos, Cheyenne did have the variable emotions of a mare. Affectionate and curious when Ed often rested on an old farm wagon. If sleeping too long or too soundly, Cheyenne would nuzzle and gently 'a just checking to see if you are alive' nudge.

Cheyenne and Sierra arrived on the farm when they were five and six years old having been separated from their mother for three years. Unfortunately Sierra was not on the farm to greet them upon their arrival.

September had developed into a wet and cool month. During the last part of the month a last storm passed over the area raining continuously throughout the day, night and into the morning of the following day. Storm effects so prevalent throughout began to lessen when daylight arrived.

Brother Don, living next door, had been feeding the farm animals in the mornings while Ed was away. Thinking that the storm had passed and in a lull void of a down pour he headed to the pasture to feed the horses. From the field shelter Pacos, Tceque, Buttermilk and Sierra came out to greet Don and have breakfast. Calm hovered and an odd silence prevailed to the point when Don had reached the steps of the house.

Instant static linked air molecules as a lighting strike linked the heavens and earth. The last lightning strike of the passing storm struck a tall jack pine and traveled down into the roots then through the moist soil to reach a twin white-pine at a sixty foot distance. Rising skyward through the trunk the cutting lightning split the V trunks apart before sparking back to the heavens.

Don shivered, crouched and turned to view the field when thunder vibrated building windows and lightning flashed brighter than a magnesium flash. Within a blink of an eye Don witnessed Pacos and Tceque kicking up hind legs and Buttermilk physically thrown twenty five feet into a muddy earth hollow filled with water. It was the heavy slump of Sanorra that caused fear in Don's mind. The path of lightning travelled from tree to tree for sixty feet beneath the earth under the area where the horses were feeding.

How lightning works is beyond the knowledge of Ed, though he speculated that the lightning split into fingers as it travelled, each finger reaching up from beneath the earth to attack each horse. Sanorra's life snatched within the seconds of the strike died instantly as the mare slumped to the ground.

This storm had sought vengeance during its' passing. Buildings, power poles, trees, the horses and two dogs a section over had been hit. Sanorra and both dogs were the only animal victims. Humans were spared, minutes and locations could have proven different. The eye of the storm arrived providing clear skies and warm sun rays to dry the earth.

Upon arriving, Ed could do nothing for Sanorra other than burry the mare where she lay. Concern was focused on the other three horses. Swollen back legs and hocks seemed to be the only minor injuries to Pacos and Tceque. Comically, though this was a tragic incident, their actions of constantly lifting back feet as if being tickled resembled horses attempting Texas line dancing. Knowing they were going to be fine Ed smiled.

Buttermilk was another matter. The mare had been hit hard and its' equilibrium had been affected. Ed and Don laboured to roll the horse out of the mud puddle and encourage the mare to stand. For the remainder of the day Ed attended to the horse by forcing it to attempt walking. Buttermilk could not walk forward in a straight line. An urge to walk backwards caused back legs to give out. A fall would be troublesome and reduce chances of recovery.

For safety when the late afternoon darkened with potential rain and impending lightning and thunder, Ed led the horses to a neighbour's building for the night. Taking up a cot for the evening, Ed cared for the three horses throughout the night as they slowly recuperated and symptoms faded. By morning, after a night of constant thundering reminders of the previous day, Pacos and Tceque seemed to be themselves though time would be needed to reduce swollen back legs. Buttermilk had stopped walking backwards though back legs and hips wobbled from side to side and would for a week or so. Ed removed mud, grim and ear puss that continuously leaked throughout the following month.

A hopeful outlook greeted the sunshine of the morning. Opening the building door, Ed led the three horses out to breath in the freshness of the beginning day. Without lead rope or halters, Ed began the short walk down the road towards home. Trailing in line, Pacos behind Ed and Tceque behind Pacos both were alert with heads high and ears perked as if nervous and anxious at the same time. Normally, without halters or lead ropes, they would wander and eat or lag back or venture ahead. Today they paraded in a straight line. Buttermilk was an exception, the mare followed at a slower pace with back end still weaving unsteadily. A constant low neigh called out to those ahead.

Ed wondered what their reaction would be when arriving at the farm and location of the lightning strike. Standing at the open gate of the fence, Ed waited, letting the horses enter at their own initiative. Pacos halted, raised a stiffened neck, its' eyes scanning the field for a sister lost, buried from sight close to the lighting stricken pine tree. Patting Pacos' neck with an understanding, Ed tightened a choked-up sensation in the throat.

Walking slowly, the gelding headed directly to a rise overlooking the surrounding area and there the old boy stayed. Eyes searched and a neighed call, which only Sanorra would answer to, moaned throughout the day. Pacos did not move, did not eat, and did not sleep. A sister, a friend would not answer to its' call.

Every herd has a leader regardless of herd numbers. Sanorra was the dominant thinking female, the leader; Pacos the silent muscle, Tceque the impatient youngster and Buttermilk the concerned mother figure. Immediately upon receiving a caressing hand along the neck, back and rump, Tceque entered the field and headed directly to the turned earth of Sanorra's grave. Sniffing around the edges and snorting as if carrying out a conversation the greyish white mare pawed the ground. Finished with its' one-sided conversation, Tceque walked around the plot then laid down and rolled three times on the soft turned sand. Standing and shaking off the sand, the mare's attitude and essence

54

changed. Tceque was now the thinking, dominant mare and leader of the herd.

Buttermilk slowly arrived at the gate and pressed its' matted white head into Ed's side under an arm. With care he wiped the runny solution of water and mud from an ear. Upon entering the field the small horse drifted between Pacos and Tceque throughout the day and neighing as if questioning the mixed-up results after a day of tragedy.

Oddness seemed to hover over the farm and the temperament of the horses was subdued. Motions of life neither unfolded without excitement nor urge to pursue new interests. Ed also seemed reluctant to do practices of the past. Pacos and Sanorra were a working team, hauling logs, pulling a carriage through tourist rides or pulling a wagon around on the farm. Though Ed harnessed Pacos in order to drag several small trees and the damaged trees hit by lightning, Pacos did not show the passion once displayed when harnessed beside Sanorra. Just thinking of the difficulty Sanorra gave when hooves needed trimming or shoeing, Ed sniffled back emotions while declaring that he missed the uncooperative mare and chores of tending to the light draft horse.

Life and excitement retuned to the ranch when the daughters of Sanorra arrived on the farm. Youthful vigour of the five and six year-old mares rejuvenated the older horses. Sierra, the all white horse displayed all of the traits of her mother. Cheyenne, the larger of the two, displayed anxiousness yet the temperament and friendliness of uncle Pacos. Buttermilk resumed the mother instincts of needing to know where the youngsters were at all times and attempted to teach the pair the etiquette of a horse. True to form, Pacos displayed an indication of bloodline and kinship. The gelding was the uncle figure and the patient teacher. All youth test authority and Cheyenne and Sierra tested Tceque. Despite being slightly larger than the Arabian-Quarter horse cross, the two youngsters were disciplined and tolerated by Tceque. As the herd leader this was Tceque's inherited job and the youngsters respected and accepted their place within the herd. Logic dictated the order of placement; Tceque, Pacos, Cheyenne, Sierra then Buttermilk. Poor Buttermilk, the mare that cares about all, the one that worries the most, the one that all turn to has the lowest standing. Ed reflected on the similarities in human society.

Scratching behind Cheyenne's ear, Ed recalled the arrival of the horse and its' sister. Both horses had settled in, Sanorra, their mother lay beneath the field at a short distance marked by a pole and a name plate. In abstract though Ed recited the selections of prose with facial expression and slight gestures suggested by the director; all with the flair of a seasoned actor. Of course the vision of grandeur was within the confines of Ed's mind.

Other than a tail swishing the odd house fly attempting to land on its' rump, Cheyenne's eyes focused on Ed's dramatic lips moving. Ears that normally rotate in random arcs, one was fixed in Ed's direction intently listening to the lilting voice of Ed spewing out prose of detached story segments. The tone and delivery of the prose must have been captivating for Cheyenne remained in place and apparently listening. Whether or not an animal understands the meanings of words of the English language is debatable.

Basic instructional words horses must understand; for words of directions allow a human and horse to work at specific jobs. If a horse is told that it is ugly or pretty, it is unlikely that the horse will know the difference. A tonal inflection when stating ugly or pretty may receive a physical reaction.

Rambling on with a flare of the dramatic, Ed finished with a pause of anticipation of applause, at least a neigh of approval or snort of distaste from Cheyenne. Tilting its' head slightly, the mare's eyes and ears expected the would-be actor to provide a reprise or encore. Sensing no further soothing words to captivate its' attention, Cheyenne lifted its' head and turned to walk away.

Dejected, Ed lifted arms in a questioning gesture to say, 'what, you did not like the performance?' Cheyenne's rump halted, its' tail raised and a pungent, aromatic gust of foul air responded to critique Ed's prose recitation and amateur performance.

Curiosity is not only a human trait, animals display curiosity within their same species and of others, and of humans. Animal curiosity may not be inherited in the same manner that humans use the function. Yet humans are animals that have advanced and have lost the basic animal instinct of using curiosity to survive.

When a dog sniffs a porcupine for the purpose of identifying the creature as a food source, it is taught that it is not food by the pain of quills thrust into the snout. Curiosity taught the dog to avoid porcupines. Some dogs just do not learn.

Young spring goats use curiosity to discover which farm animals are safe to play with. The farm goose is a good play-pal if a game of chase is selected. Horses, not so much, their large feet are dangerous. When a horse is lying down then they do not mind a baby goat climbing about or sleeping next to their warm body.

Suckling a cow's utter just because of the size and abundance of milk should only be dreamed of. An unwanted goat expressing curiosity will be kicked away by a hoof as large as a goat's head.

Though the herd ram seems aloft and coldly dominant it will always allow the young kids to butt his head and climb about.

Chickens do not like to play with goats and will flap wings and squawk. Roosters attack and kick claws at inquisitive faces.

On a visit to the farm in late fall when Canadians decide it is time to wear toques, a young nephew of five years of age arrived bundled up in winter clothes including warm boots and suitable for puddle jumping, mitts for warmth, a toque over ears and covered by a hood of a warm coat. Young Steven waddled about with curiosity following Uncle Ed going about farm chores. At five years of age a child is of no assistance physically, yet they are curious.

Leaning forward with hands on knees Steven blankly watched Uncle trimming Pacos' hooves. The kid's face expressed no animation yet the eyes widened and absorbed the strange procedure of Uncle and Pacos' interacting. Ed squatted forward with Pacos' front hoof on a peg stand. Filing the excess rim of the hoof to make it smooth and round, Ed's neck and shoulders squirmed as Pacos' lips nibbled the nap of his neck. Steven giggled when Pacos' big lips played with the wool ball on Uncle's toque. Then Pacos mouthed the ball and pulled the toque off. Uncle pulled it back; Pacos pulled it off, Uncle pulled it back. Over and over the fight for possession continued, all the while Steven laughed at the pair's playful antics.

Though near as close as could be Steven's curiosity about the craft of trimming and shoeing of a horse was not important, Uncle was not important. The big playful horse doing everything to tease Uncle was important. Pacos knew when to pull the toque off, when to tickle Uncle's neck, when to wait for Uncle to pull the toque down, when to just play with the wool ball then just at the right moment pull the toque off and shake it about just out of Uncle's reach. Steven heartily laughed without moving from his crunched stance. Laughter only erupted after the toque was pulled off.

Steven's face showed no indication of Pacos' action for Uncle to view. Nephew was communicating with Pacos by not showing any facial reactions of what Pacos was about to do. When Ed glanced to Steven, the child's eyes blankly met his with no clue of what might happen. A burst of laughter erupted from the silent kid when Pacos successfully accomplished pulling Ed's toque off and keeping it out of reach.

Finishing with the front hooves, Ed moved to the back and out of reach of Pacos' big lips. Disappointed that the teasing was over Steven stood and stayed at the front staring up at the big horse. Lowering its' head so that big dark eyes stared directly into Steven's there was a transfer of communication. Steven shrugged shoulders as if disappointed that the teasing was over.

Sensing that Ed was relaxed and confident that he would no longer be bothered Pacos flapped a lower lip at Steven then reached its' neck back towards Ed's turned back. Hunched over with the horse's back leg between legs and resting on knees Ed commenced flat filing the hoof. Pacos' lips stretched toward gloves sticking out of Ed's back pocket. Gently Pacos nibbled with lips then fixed a hold between teeth and withdrew the gloves. Steven's face grimaced with delight, impressed by Pacos' ability to pick pocket Uncle.

Turning to the front, Pacos waited, held head still with an eye captivating Steven's stare. Both held still until Ed lowered the horse's leg and stepped to the front to retrieve the gloves. Just at the right moment Pacos shook its' head up and down and tossed the gloves at the maximum height of the lift. Following the sail of the gloves in opposite directions Steven laughed. When Ed semi-smirked a smile and a frown to Pacos and accomplice, Steven just shrugged as if to say, 'I had no part of this!'

Though being an adult and at an age that younger people consider beyond having the ability of curiosity, Ed is as curious as any child. The difference between old and young is that the young are just visual sponges absorbing content. An adult will mentally contemplate, question and even have a one-sided telepathic conversation. Whether or not an animal or vegetation converses is a matter for theorists to study.

What manner of intelligence does Pacos posses in the ability to create teasing? Some may state that it is in a horse's nature to assume that food is in need of tasting. Ed's toque and gloves are potential food substances. Hog wash! Maybe, when a first taste is required? Surely Pacos knows that leather gloves and a wool toque are not food. A one time occurrence . . . possibly the food analogy would be acceptable. Pacos repeats the actions time and time again, and even goes out of its' way, often sneaking up upon Ed in order to steel the toque or gloves. Intelligence and play is not limited to the human race.

When the coolness of fall arrives on mornings when the fallen leaves crunch under foot then the urge to hunt stimulates the mind. Rabbit season opening lured Ed out of a warm bed and into the cedar swamps in search of scampering jackrabbits. Pleasurable walking in the bush is surreal in the fall. After all there is no black flies or northern dive-bombing mosquitoes to slap, scratch or run from and escape to the security of the indoors.

Sound of silence is the un-distributable sounds of creatures going about daily existence. Squirrels sit on haunches nibbling on pine cones and fill cheeks with seeds. When filled they search for a hiding place to store the stash. Fifty percent of the time a squirrel will forget where it stashed the bounty. Often a fellow squirrel or observant chipmunk will procure the fellow creature's winter provisions.

Standing on a trail listening for the plop-plop of rabbit hops, Ed glanced upward to see the hints of winter lightly falling. Specks of snow floated down, just enough to veil the view in Three-D perspective of the cedar swamp. Cradled in folded arms, Ed's twenty-two's cold barrel pointed at a skewed angle. In a flutter of wings chickadees hopped from alder branches to alder branches in search of lingering bugs. In the midst of foraging, a curious chickadee lands on the tip of the rifle barrel and stares into Ed's squinting eyes. A twitch of a smile turns up on one side of Ed's lips.

Has the chickadee ever seen a human before or is it curious, or by random chance needed to rest on the rifle barrel or considers the cold metal to be just another tree branch? In return did the chickadee offer a pleased curious expression? Having studied each other for an extended moment the little brown and white breasted bird flew off to trail behind a disappearing flock.

As soon as the snow began to fall giving a hint of what the winter months would bring, the crystals vanished. Marvelling on the encounter with the small bird, Ed continued along the shore of a beaver pond, thoughts not on the rabbit hunt. Odds are that several camouflaged rabbits watched the human creature walk by. Continuing along the shore, Ed's direction was a water link between an upper beaver pond and a lower pond. Snaking through a low land area the creek's banks held jack pines and alders with a haunting density.

A different sound, a muffled forest sound prevailed within the bush and allowed filtered-in sounds of the flowing creek water and distant water fowl to penetrate. Sitting on a log, Ed crossed the rifle upon his lap and bending forward stared into the creek water calmed by a shore inlet. Lost in abstract thought that had nothing to do with hunting, the forest or the flowing water, Ed really had no idea what meanings his thoughts invoked. This is called communing with nature, doing nothing, not moving, not thinking, just existing and encompassed by nature.

At moments like this is when the unexpected unfolds, where the difference between species becomes unimportant, mutually safe and will allow curiosity. As if instantly appearing out of nowhere, this is Ed's point of view, a young female deer lowered its' head into Ed's peripheral sight. Less than three feet to the side the light brown deer pressed its muzzle to the water and sucked up cool liquid. A dark eye watched Ed's head slightly turn and the human's eyes inspected the situation. Without flinching the deer drank until satisfied then lifted its' head to view Ed with both eyes. Each studied the other. Ed could have reached out to touch the warm hair on the deer's shoulder. In return the deer began to stretch its neck in a contemplation of sniffing or licking the human. Rather both continued to visually inspect the other. If only verbal communication could have commenced.

What knowledge could have been gained, an exchange of questions and answers that would change previous conceptions? At a point where the meeting has not provided an exchange of thoughts, rather only a visual interpretation, the deer turned and took several steps. Hesitating it turned its' head slightly back, maybe anticipating a breakthrough in communication, then disappointingly disappeared within two graceful leaps. Not an echo of branches or breaking twigs cracking sounded nor footfalls in the moss covered ground had indicated the existence of the deer's visit.

The moment was a fragment of time shared only between the deer and human. Did a squirrel, beaver, bird or another deer or human witness the encounter? Ed felt privileged yet saddened that the emotion could not be shared. In this age of instant video recording devices and media sharing there are numerous visual encounters being displayed. They are only visual. Ed and the deer shared transference of personal substance that cannot be shared or understood by others.

A flash back of the deer encounter surfaced in Ed's mind as he watched a young Steven communicating with Pacos. Steven was not speaking in a six-year-olds' language to Pacos, he was communicating with body language. Antics of Steven's bundled up body was an indication of play, to play with Pacos in the way Pacos played with Ed. The massive horse towered over the small boy, its' eyes inquisitive about the little human creature.

Bundled in a toque with a hood of a coat over the head and oversized mitts covering small hands, Steven stepped closer to large legs. Unsure of the small version of Ed, Pacos tilted its' head to focus eyes in a questioning manner, asking, 'what is this kid doing, what does he want?' Steven turned his back to Pacos and began to back against the unmoveable tree-trunk legs.

Ed watched, yet waited without attempting to question Steven's intent. Despite the abundance of Pacos, Ed knew the temperament of the horse and of the safe encounter between human and equine. As if cluing in on the human's intent, Pacos' lips licked the hood of Steven's coat. It was not a toque and there was no wool pomp-pomp to sustain its' interest. Steven's face held an unconcerned frown. Ed assumed that Steven and Pacos lacked mutual understanding.

After a hesitation with no interactive play, Pacos parted lips and teeth grasping a mouthful of the hood material began lifting. Steven's face disappeared into the coat, arms folded inward, legs and body seemed to stretch until the child's whole body lifted clear of the ground. Ed's eyes widened and he pushed away from the fence. He was tempted to scold Pacos, yet refrained when the horse lowered the child back onto feet.

Feet settled and gained balance before Pacos released the hood. Lips smacked in an effort to release the taste of the multi-blend of man made fabric. Ed noticed a familiar snicker from Pacos, the same one after stealing a toque or gloves. Steven's arms relaxed and the coat slowly assumed a normal fit. A face began to fill the emptiness of the hood. A toque appeared, furrowed eye brows, small wide dark eyes then a wide smile of pleasure and satisfaction as if to say, 'this is much better than having a toque pulled off.' Ed smirked before relaxing against the fence rail.

Turning to face Pacos, Steven stared up at a large head bobbing up and down, as if indicating pleasure from the encounter. 'This is cool,' filled Steven's thoughts. Turning around, Steven backed beneath Pacos' head, tightened arms and waited for another lift.

9

Though the colours of brown, dark brown, black and darker tinges seem to be the standard pigmentations of horses, Ed preferred the lighter versions. All of the horses residing on 'Sanora's Siesta and Ranch' were of the lighter tones and shades. Tceque, an Arabian-Quarter horse cross had a white coat with black main, forelock and black tail. A slow change from white to grey-black blended from the hock to hoof. A satin white coat is the best description of colour and feel of Tceque's coat.

Due to the type of training the mare received for carriage work and discipline training among police horses gave the mare a standing of inelegance. Probably holding a higher inelegance than other resident horses, well mannered, accepted directions and fulfilled the commands without hesitation. A dependable horse, though Ed believed that the training robbed the horse of a free personality.

Take Pacos, a teasing, playful and an affectionate gelding that would nuzzle a head onto a human, Cheyenne also, yet Tceque would not. A pat on the nose or gentle grooming was accepting, though the mare would not interact; rather stand stiffly as if being snobbish. The mare was not snobbish, just well trained. If Pacos was to take on the persona of an entertainer then Tceque evoked the head mistress of a household staff.

Unlike having the presence of Sanora to be a leader, Tceque's training elevated the mare to leader after Sanora's passing. The importance of leadership may not be of importance, yet it allows the leader to eat and drink first and accept the first taste of sweet feed and treats. In return the leader makes the decisions as to when to eat, rest and what part of the pastures to use.

After the loss of Sanora, Buttermilk easily accepted Tceque as the new leader. Pacos seemed to be withdrawn by the loss of a sister and moped around until gaining its' playfulness again. Being a playful individual, the gelding easily accepted Tceque burdening the leadership roll. When Cheyenne and Sierra arrived, they had no choice in accepting Tceque's guidance, Pacos' experiences and Buttermilk's mothering.

Age creeps up on everyone and also on horses at double the rate. Joints move slower, the sheen of colour diminishes and weight fluctuates and then suddenly the horse is old. At that point the horse is retired. Tceque no longer pulled a carriage, nor was ridden. Tceque, Pacos and Buttermilk were within a year or two of age and were considered seniors. When in a herd each looks out for the other and Ed has to be able to pay attention to differences in personalities.

Ed noticed a change in attitude in the farm animals on a warm May morning. An unusual warm spring had brought the vegetation up and every insect into full force. When all animals should have been out in the pastures, the goats hung close to the barn, several horses stood in a disorganized gathering. Even No-Frills, a Hereford-Charolias cow cross stood on the pathway staring towards the back section of the farm.

An animal was missing. In hindsight Ed recalled not seeing all of the animals the night before. Animals have a routine and as usual return to the barn by late afternoon and rest before wandering at night after the insects become less aggressive. Ed did not see Tceque last night. This morning the mare was not about. The remainder of stock seemed disorganized as if left without instructions by their leader.

This was a fact; Tceque was not about and had been since a last sighting a morning earlier. A strange sensation flushed through Ed starting with a cool shiver then a swell of heat about the head. At anytime of worry concern and fear, Ed's body and mind becomes overwhelmed. Always the worst is expected, a fabricated scenario plays out in abstract thoughts. Blood rushes through veins and movements become agitated. No-Frills the cow stood facing the road leading to the back section. Further up Sierra and Cheyenne waited, each facing the same direction.

Ed's heart muscles flexed and pumped blood in pulsations into his head when rushing up to talk to the horses. They seemed to display the same concern. Walking past in a general direction, the same direction Cheyenne's head pointed, Ed crested the rise of earth looking down over a gully where the creek passed through. Late spring had diverted most of the heavy winter accumulation of water. Low lands still held a high saturation point.

Cheyenne and Ed peered through brush to see Tceque's head bobbing, a repeating action to ward off pesky flies. Heat and moisture of the low areas hold an abundance of pesky bugs created to annoy man and beast. Only the white of Tceque's head, neck and back reflected above the dark earth. Ed wondered why the mare was lying down. Of course the worst of thoughts enters the mind. Why would a horse be lying down, because the mare suffered colic? No, a colic horse would be rolling in an attempt to dislodge an obstruction, then a broken leg? Of course, it had to be a broken leg. Tceque broke a leg and fell then rolled down the incline into the bog of the gully.

Rushing along the road leading to the creek, Ed hurried to Tceque's aid with Cheyenne following at rushing heels. All night Tceque lay here alone without help. Though the other animals held concern they were unable to open a gate and knock on the house door and inform Ed of a situation. A previous memory flashed through Ed's mind of the time he himself was in peril and only the horses were around to witness, though they were concerned they were unable to assist.

Only humans can verbally communicate and mentally and physically assist those in distress. Ed has witnessed a mother cow attempting to assist a calf in distress, but physically is unable to verbally and physically seek assistance. In Ed's case when alone in the bush without prior knowledge to others and without communication devices, a human is as vulnerable as an animal.

Before the heat allowed insects to densely fill the bush, warm spring days required Ed to inspect the property fences. Spring runoff worked correctly this particular year. Snow melt was evenly dispensed by evaporation, melting and seepage into the ground and creeks. Through the land where the fence line ran along raised land, swampy areas and the water shed, the earth was dry though the creeks were flowing to a brim capacity.

Only a half mile from the house and neighbours mingling and within sight of farm animals feeding, Ed was essentially alone, not missed. Heading down a gully slope, Ed followed the electric fence to the flowing creek where the line crossed. All wires and connections were good. Step across the three foot wide creek and only two miles of fence to check.

A three foot wide creek with solid earth on both sides is an easy leap, not even a leap, just a long stride. Why stride, why leap when stepping on a fallen log acting as a bridge would be easier. Logic defines that a leap or stride may encounter an unsecured landing on the opposite side. A bridge does not require chance or undue physical leaping to cross. Ed took the easy and less flare approach to crossing the little creek. A first test step on the six inch diameter birch log responded with a solid texture. A second step added weight and was secure.

Knowledge of trees, weathering and degradation due to age and type of wood fibre under stress should have been pre-determined before advancing. On the way down under the muted cracking sound of the rotten log breaking the strength analysis was confirmed. Though too late to react, Ed's body sunk beneath the water. A cold shiver worked its' way up from toes to knees, to groin and inched past the belly button.

There seemed to be no bottom in the three foot wide creek. It was surprising how fast the mind thinks and the body reacts to distressed situations. Ed's mind instructed eyes to search for possible support, for arms to reach out and latch onto brush, for muscles to tense and pull. As quickly as the fall occurred the body responded with hands latching onto brush and arm muscles lifting Ed's body out of the cold bath water.

Legs and feet had pushed and kicked to no avail. They had not reached the bottom of the creek. A stronger water flow, a missed grab for support, unsupportable brush, or a sideways fall and no one would have responded to Ed's water gobbled calls for help. The distance was only a half mile from home.

Though spring and a warm sunny day with a temperature pushing eighteen degrees Celsius, this was not swimming weather. A cold penetrated skin and muscles and wet clothing hung with water. Quickly Ed shed rubber boots and striped off clothing in order to absorb the sun's heat filtering through the early leafing on brush and trees.

If only the embarrassment of walking home naked was a story to be told, Ed resigned himself to accept the snickers. A possible tragic outcome would not be a story told by others. Emptying rubber boots of water, ringing out socks and clothing and rubbing excess moisture from his body, Ed finally relaxed with a core warming. Stepping into wet rubber boots and with bundled clothes in arms, Ed walked a-la-natural back towards home. Ed would swear that there were smirks on faces and commenting thoughts in the farm animals' minds as he paraded past.

Arriving at the bottom of the road where the creek exited the bog of the gully, Ed came face to face with Tceque's situation. The elderly mare had not fallen nor had broken a leg. With an ingrained need to eat, the mare's walking progressively led Tceque into the boggy area. Shear weight of a horse on legs designed for walking and running forced the hooves into the saturated earth. The downward suction of mud swallowed the legs up to the buoyancy of the horse's stomach.

Tceque was stuck and unable to move legs. Upper body movement struggled to move thus draining reserved strength. Age also hindered stamina and the promise of successful recovery.

Having placed a call to the veterinary, Ed rushed back to Tceque with the old nineteen fifty-seven ford tractor and a rope-haul harness. Placing logs onto the bog, Ed reached Tceque and reassured the mare with words of comfort and brushing of eyes and ears. Driving an arm into the wet mud, Ed's hand drew the rope under Tceque's chest and behind front legs. Harnessed to prevent injury and attached to the tractor, Ed began to reduce slack in the rope. Under low gear the tractor strained to break the suction power of the mud and wet clay mixture.

A slurping sound indicated that the horse had been pulled free. Once onto dry ground, Ed inspected Tceque for injuries. Old age had taken the bulk of fitness and lasting stamina from the mare. The nightlong struggle reduced the last resources available for recovery. Unable to stand despite assistance, Ed soothed the tired mare with head caressing while the vet administered a humane dispatching dose.

From the rise overlooking the bog, Cheyenne watched until Ed covered the mare with a blanket. Though at this time only Cheyenne, Sierra, two cows, four goats, poultry and fowl remained on the farm, Cheyenne accepted leadership.

10

Sometimes different species tolerate each other, sometimes show respect and even domesticated farm animals and wild life live among the other. Often wild ducks will land among the domestic, swim in the same pond, yet just at a respectful distance. If feed is tossed, the domestic eat first, the wild eat at the fringes and peck at leftovers when the domestic are full and have waddled off.

Wild geese are summoned by the deep throaty honk of the domestic white, often visiting in the early morning. In silence they wander the pasture unmolested while four-legged animals grasp extended sleep. Of the rare visitors is a resident pair of Sand Hill Cranes. Over the years the pair has raised pairs of gangly youngsters, seldom seen though glimpses occur of long legged shadows walking through the bush. The odd sight of sticks walking, yes, their legs resemble slender trunks of young saplings uprooted and taking a leisured stroll. Blinking and second thoughts are needed to dispense the illusion of saplings walking about the woods.

Most illusive is a Great Grey Heron. Where it lives, or where its' nest is, is a mystery. The heron has been around for years, so many years that Ed assumes that it is pre-historic. There is no way to tell if it is male of female. There may be a pair though only one is ever seen at one viewing. A pair has only been seen on a spring arrival or on a fall departure. From high above against the blue of the sky a brown shadow of a six foot wing span a Heron glides on invisible air currents. With such a wing span how could long legs, long neck and wide wings land feet first into a kiddies pool sized pond? Yet it does and lands without a sound and when startled takes flight without a flutter of noise.

Gertrude and Heathcliff, the resident white geese are the watchers of the farm. They are the ones that notice all arrivals and departures of winged visitors and land prowlers. Their distinctive geese honks, with a varied vocal delivery, inform residents and Ed of arrivals, departures and the identity of species.

Crows, Ravens, Buzzards, Sand Hill Cranes, Great Grey Heron, Ducks and Geese receive a friendly hello and goodbye honk. Owls, Hawks, Falcons; those birds of prey that sneak around in search of a free meal will receive a blasting scornful honk. Despite the varied farm species all seem to understand the distress warning from the geese.

There are always going to be snoopers when domesticated farm animals are viewed as easy pickings. Though the farm animals are protected in-doors at night does not mean that prowlers do not sniff around under the cover of darkness. On a steady rotation on a journey through its' territory a local fox will checkout the hen house or peek into the barn. The looming shape of a cow in the shadows of the dark makes a fox think twice.

Gertrude lays eggs every spring, yet despite the efforts of Heathcliff and Gertrude, creating a family has been illusive. Even fowl suffer conception problems that humans experience. Humans make a conscious decision to adopt. Geese do not seek out orphaned geese and do not go searching for an alternative outside of their species.

Orphans exist and based on the rule of letting nature take its' course, most young do not survive especially at an immature age. There are compassionate city folks that cannot understand the rule of letting nature take its' course. Sometimes unnecessary rescues of wayward fowl create orphans that are brought to the local humane society. Those that show signs of survival often are delivered to Ed. In turn Ed releases self-sufficient juvenile to the various beaver ponds on the farm. Relative wild security and mingling of like species the young thrive and adapt to the freedom of the wild.

On occasion an orphan arrives that imprints on humans. A young wild gosling arrived and had attached itself to Ed. The immature Canada goose followed Ed around the farm, always at Ed's heels. Heathcliff eyed the youngster with cautious indifference. To say that Heathcliff did not want anything to do with the gosling is a contradiction. A concerned eye watched where the youngster went and a scornful honk would scold the wayward goose. On the other hand, Gertrude seemed to accept the orphan and offered guidance, more of a big sister teaching the gosling the ways of a goose. Similarities of wild and domestic geese are prevalent and would provide a basis for the gosling to work from.

Despite what do-gooders from the city think is happening, based on their Disney fantasy thoughts of everlasting happiness for the rescued orphan, Ed knows better. The gosling needed to experience and learn to be a wild goose. If not learning to fend for itself, it would perish. Living with Gertrude and Heathcliff should only be temporary, an intern timeframe before moving on. The natural instinct of the wildness for a goose is to seek out its' own kind did not develop in the gosling.

Full feathering and colour distinction developed on the gosling and a mature size indicated maturing. Ed shooed and chased the youngster, an attempt to teach the goose to fly. It would flap wings and slap feet against the ground in a running gate of the flightless domestic geese, but would not fly. Gertrude would honk and the wild goose would waddle back to its' adoptive parents.

Frowning with an expression of frustration, Ed picked up the goose laying at rest at his feet and carried it down the farm road toward the beaver pond a quarter mile at the back south-east corner of the property. Acting in a typical tourist sightseeing manner, the goose twisted its' head up, down, right, left, forward and back taking in the landscape and changing scenery. There is a road, bush, a clearing, the typical farm junk yard, the fork in the road, more bush, and then the large beaver pond. Each new feature the goose's wide brown eyes took in.

From a pocket Ed removed feed and placed it on a mound overlooking the pond then placed the goose down. A bewildered goose eyed the pond to the right, left then looked up at Ed. Ed talks to animals no differently than talking to humans and in a soothing conversational voice described the goose's new home. Attention to dangers, the best place to sleep at night and where the best food is located, Ed suggested before bidding the goose goodbye.

At a distance up the road rising away from the pond, Ed turned back with an expectation of seeing the goose eagerly swimming in the pond. Disappointment showed on Ed's face bristling with greying beard hair. There on the mound in the same position sat the goose, its' head quizzically eyeing the deep dark water. Ed waited hoping that the goose would not look in his direction. With a hastened pace Ed headed back to the farm.

Over the following three days Ed wandered back to the beaver pond to check up on the goose and leave a ration of feed on a first visit. Worry filled Ed's thoughts when seeing the original feed untouched. When scanning the quarter acre pond and the upper pond of the same size the goose could not be spotted. The worst of results were pictured; a dead goose floating in the pond, bleached bones on the shore or an injured goose cowering with fright in the bush.

Honking with imitation similarity to a goose call, Ed's voice echoed over the pond. Not hearing a response he called again and again. Then a faint reply sounded from within the bush, a fair distance from the pond. Carrying on a back and forth conversation, Ed concluded that the goose was fine. In turn the goose knew of Ed's concern. Why the goose was in the bush was questioned, though Ed assumed that the goose was just feeding on grass.

Day two found the goose deeper in the bush and further from the pond. Maybe the goose did not like deep water, for the pond at the farm was not deep and easily crossed by wading. On day three no reply came from the goose. In hopeful conclusion Ed decided that the goose tired of the bush and took flight out of necessity and joined a flock of geese on the next farm.

Accepting that the goose had adapted to the wilder side of life, Ed did not visit the pond the next day, resigning to concentrate on repairs in the shop. Rising from under the tractor and hitching up pants refusing to be supported by worn out suspenders, eyes glared out through the open ended repair shed.

Standing firmly in front, staring with beady eyes, the wild goose faced Ed down. There were no sounds of honking or fluttering of wings to indicate the goose's arrival. Placing hands on hips Ed approached the goose and confronted the condemning stare. Ed eyed the goose which seemed road worn. Feathers were dry and frayed, the white neck patch speckled with brush burrs and webbed feet were caked with dry mud and dusty sand. The goose did not fly home . . . it walked the long way, a three day, one mile journey through the bush until finding the farm road. Familiarity of land mark sights observed the first day guided the goose home.

Both stared, no talking, no honking, and neither one backing away from the confrontation. Ed offered a welcome home and stated that the goose would have to make its' own decisions. Three beak gestures, the goose's equivalent of an accepting nod, and a gurgled response it accepted Ed's greeting. Turning, the goose headed to the small pond and greeted Gertrude floating about. From the side Heathcliff sounded one guttural acknowledging honk.

Gertrude became a stand-in mother figure for the wild goose though unable to truly provide a wild teaching. On the other hand Heathcliff tolerated the wild goose and showed no affection, no father figure teachings of life. Yet an instinct of geese is to be a protector and watchdog for the farm and the animals contained within farm confines. Always watching the perimeter of the farm Heathcliff noticed a brown shaped movement at the south fence. A whiskered face stared between the fence wires, its' eyes surveying the smorgasbord of food varieties. The non-native bobcat sniffed in the smells of lunch.

Stretching up a long neck, Heathcliff's blue eyes accounted for the location of all farm animals under its' watch. Goats snoozed in the warm sun by the barn. Chickens pecked within chicken runs. Stunned turkeys chased a single moth within the turkey pen. Gertrude wadded in the stale water of the pond. All domestics were accounted for and for the moment were safe. An informational honk alerted all; heads turned, ears perked and goat noses sniffed the air.

Bending low to the ground front paws eased the bobcat's body under the electric fence wire. Open space of the pasture needed to be crossed before reaching the easy prey of unaware chickens. The cat would have to rush and pounce quickly in order to reduce being noticed. A dark form off to the aside caught the cat's attention. A white neck patch bobbed and its' beak busy nibbling on grass.

Lost in its' need to feed the wild goose lacked defensive training. It had paid no attention to Gertrude's honk, a honk beckoning wayward goslings. Lost meanings in translation left the wild goose in harms way. Repeated honks turned to scolding then to pleading to be understood. Even the deeper honk from Heathcliff went unnoticed.

A flicker of paws dashing across the pasture forced Heathcliff's orange webbed feet to pad across the field. Wings flapped to aid in an aggressive attack on the invading carnivore. Midway between the wild goose and the fence Heathcliff and the bobcat collided. Heathcliff pecked and slapped wings in an offensive defence of the wild goose.

Bewildered by the blindsided attack the bobcat rolled onto its' back and reacted with a snapping jaw and clutching front legs hugging its' assailant. Odds of surprise may have startled the bobcat but the cat's killing instinct surpassed Heathcliff's brave attack. Canine teeth sliced through neck feathers and the cat's muscled jaw crushed bone and severed neck joints.

Instantly Heathcliff's honking was silenced, replaced by the wild goose's startled honking and Gertrude's confused calls. Gertrude and the wild goose huddled in the little pond and watched with disbelief as the bobcat dragged Heathcliff under the fence and disappear behind the dense wall of the forest.

All animals remained close to the security of pens, houses and ponds for the remainder of the day. Secured for the night the reminders of the day's turmoil faded. By morning all would be forgotten and farm life would continue. Not for Gertrude, continuous calls for Heathcliff's return sounded for three days, three days of mourning.

A year later when the wild goose reached maturity it took flight and joined a flock of transient geese. Gertrude raised the orphan well. Heathcliff, though less affectionate towards the wild goose, fought to save the gosling and paid the price with its' life.

All creatures seem to depend on each other in one way or another. Gertrude was at a loss without Heathcliff and the wild goose. Of all the critters on the farm, Gertrude selected Buttercup, a two year old cow to hang around with. When the large Charolais-Red Angus cross ventured about the farm, waddling legs would rush to follow. When napping, Gertrude would nest close by. Buttercup accepted and understood Gertrude's need for companionship and was the only farm animal that would allow Gertrude to peck at bugs and grass beneath its' belly and through legs.

Each spring Gertrude accepted orphaned geese from the humane society and nurtured them until each ventured back into the wild. Each fall Buttercup and Gertrude resumed their companionship.

Life on the farm has the impression of tranquillity yet wild life is present in abundance. Most of the time domestic and wild animals cohabitate without intermingling. At times the carnivore species linger within sniffing distance and the lure of easy pickings entice wild carnivores to partake of an available and fuss-free meal. Domesticated animals do not always flee; their flight mechanisms have been removed or pacified by conditioning.

A pair of Sand Hill Cranes and young walking through may only receive a passing glance of inquisitive stares at long spindle legs stepping gingerly in a purposeful direction. Wild geese and ducks often do not receive a second glance unless approaching feed stations then the domestic will protect their feed source.

11

An odd occurrence for most farm animals and even for Ed was to see a rarely seen snapping turtle venture onto the farm road. For a species that spends ninety percent of its' time in water, the need to lay eggs required the rare land visit. This one foot diameter shelled amphibian must have been twenty years of age. Disregarding the eyes of the curious the female turtle selected a soft sandy spot on the edge of the road to dig an egg nest. Hind feet scraped a cavity suitable to incubate its' eggs and over a time frame of six hours eggs slowly accumulated.

Watching from a respectable distance, Ed teared up when seeing teardrops forming and dropping from the turtle's eyes. Tears caused by labouring pain or tears expressed for the future generation that will hatch and struggle in a singular way to survive.

Once the eggs were covered with sand the turtle tiredly travelled through the bush to the creek and disappeared into the murky waters. Over the summer months Ed checked the nest location. To his dismay no hatchlings emerged from the sand. No new generation to populate the creek and ponds.

During many travels about the farm, along creek and pond banks, Ed wondered how many turtles occupied the waterways. Sights were few and far between. A small snapper had been seen near the pasture in a little mud puddle. A box turtle has been seen each August crossing the pasture heading towards the south wooded area. Maybe it is a female going to lay eggs or a male making a yearly amorous engagement?

Though the farm is not considered bordering the secluded wilds, wildlife that are not considered rural residents do visit and have adapted cohabitation within the farm vicinity. It is a matter of being in the right place at the right time, or just plain luck must occur in order to sight the rare animals. Manoeuvring about the land without haste and with respect; both eyes and ears and senses must be acute and animals will be encountered.

Being in the right spot at the right time is just luck. Ed had farm chores to complete, yet declined to move from leaning against the corner of the barn. Just a second to contemplate the solitude of the moment was required. Some might claim that Ed was daydreaming. The afternoon was near its' end when the sun begins to indicate the end of August. Animals had been fed and bedded down for the night. Cows, goats and horses were still out in the field and had not begun to migrate towards the barn area. Stillness prevailed around the barn's yard area.

In that moment of appreciating the quiet moment and being thankful for existence, Ed told himself to move, continue chores, yet stayed put. A distant shadow, moving at the end of the yard bordered by spacious trees and an open path leading down to the north pasture, caught Ed's eye. 'Just a horse,' assumed Ed until the shadow did not produce the white colouring of resident horses. A dark brown body supported on long spindle legs stepped up into the clearing. A majestic creature, though not considered the prettiest of the Cervidae family, the Moose demands respect.

Having seen moose on previous occasions, this sight still evoked amazement. Ed's wide eyes framed the majestic stance, the broad chest, long beard indicating age, droopy snout and massively wide antlers. Amazingly the animal approached the clearing without the rack colliding with trees and branches, nor emitting an audible sound.

At any given time Ed can hear the cows, horses and goats at a distance in the bush without the ability to visually see them. Domestic animals have decided that protection from predators is provided by their masters, so there is no need to be stealth.

Cautious yet not in worry, the moose stood in portrait profile, its' massive head slowly panning to allow beady black eyes to encompass the clearing. Could it have been the slight tilt of Ed's white cowboy hat or eyeballs adjusting for clarity of view that the moose noticed. All animals focus on the eyes of other animals, a means of telling if an animal will flee or attack. Eye movement reveals intended body movements. Boxers study the eyes of opponents for slight eye movements, iris contraction and expanding will indicate intended body movements.

Both creatures using their own understanding of self-existence attempted to understand the other. Eyes stared and minds functioned to understand the rare meeting of species. Time lasted longer than the actual time lapse and Ed wished that an extended encounter could have been sustained. Neither participant had moved from a frozen position.

With curiosity satisfied the moose casually turned and retraced its' arrival and disappeared. Its' slender hind end with grey leg hairs was the last sight seen by Ed. Pleased by the encounter he was disappointed that a longer in-depth time frame could not have been extended. The movement was over with no physical documentation to verify the encounter. Memories can be recalled over and over and enjoyment gained by the recall. Lacking the ability to recall is a disability equal to various physical disabilities, a hindrance to a person. Will the moose always be able to recall this encounter? Is the moose self-aware of self-existence?

Fall arrived on the farm and the barnyard inhabitants began to adapt to weather changes. When a covering of snow hid the wilted grass, hay became their source of dietary intake. At the first light of lengthening darkened hours animals gathered at the feeders waiting for Ed to arrive and dispense feed rations.

Unlike privileged domestic animals wildlife did not have an Ed to provide their winter food. Daily scavenging can be rewarding or days of hunger can be experienced when food sources become limited. Forage feeders and insect consuming animals may experience reduced shortages though do not experience extended durations that carnivores experience. A bear hibernates to bypass the need to forage and a need to eat constantly. A draw back is being plump in fall and skinny in spring. For those carnivores that do not hibernate must hunt. If and when passing by domestic dwellings, or knowing where domestic animals congregate, carnivores will take advantage of selecting easy prey.

Man is a carnivore and partakes of hunting in the same manner as wild predators. Raising food for self consumption seems to be socially acceptable. There may be those people of a vegetarian persuasion who will condemn those that are only practicing what is inherently natural to mankind. Very few carnivore humans condemn the chosen life style of vegetarians. To harvest from nature is as natural as farming and harvesting domesticated animals.

Man can suffer the same setbacks as wild carnivores. A day of hunting can be fruitless; a week can be just as fruitless. Being in the forest on a hunt is utopia and in a way satisfying an ancient ritual of man searching for food to feed self and family. Modern man unsuccessful during a hunt can return home and satisfy hunger by selecting pre-packaged foods from cupboards. Wildlife cannot return to the den hungry for there are no food storages waiting.

A low fog misted through the forest two feet above a wet blanket of snow. Above the six-foot depth of fog cold air threatened to bring snow. Rising slowly in the eastern sky a red tinged sun struggled to heat up the late fall day. Out early, Ed trudged through the wet layers of snow searching for active rabbit trails. Other carnivores were also out on the hunt. Fox prints followed a set trail using the same path Ed had blazed during the summer. A lynx track leaped back and forth across the trail to sniff for fresh rabbit scents.

Both fox and lynx had passed through late the previous evening or early this morning before shadows were awakened. Rabbits had moved about during the darkness of night when a crust had formed on the snow's surface. Few prints had broken through the crust; where as fox and lynx prints sat below the surface. Yet Ed sensed that he was not alone in the forest this morning. A silence prevailed; birds were not chirping or fluttering from branch to branch. Squirrels were nesting waiting for the sun to warm up the air. Chipmunks yawned and stretched within burrows under the snow; yet Ed was not alone. Other creatures were moving about in silence.

Bending below the mist in order to scan the surface of the snow, eyes squinted, a method of picking out rabbits hopping on scented trails. The whiteness of fur associated with the snow would not have completely changed on the rabbits' winter coat. Patches of white blotched on the sandy brown fur of summer. Nothing moved across the landscape of twigs emerging from within the snow and disappearing into the void of the mist.

Shadows moved at Ed's peripheral, shadows as misty as the fog. Ghostly figures of silent movement hovered and floated between snow and mist. Seldom seen, nor documented with a denial of habituating south of the forty-ninth parallel, a pair of Northern Wolves crossed Ed's sight. Only a brief encounter happened, just an eye to eye indication that the other existed. Limited depth of vision due to the thickness of moisture affected by warm air and a cold snow surface allowed Ed to follow the wolves' path. A lifetime of anticipation of such an encounter lasted a brief moment of time, yet a fixed vision is implanted into the mind to be recalled over and over. Hope for a repeat meeting was longed for the instant Ed's vision ended.

Huddled motionless in the snow, only eyes darted along the blurred horizon. Lifting his toque above ears Ed strained to hear sounds. No footfalls of paws could be heard only the slight breathing indication of excitement contained within Ed's body. This is the extent of any visual display of excitement Ed would offer when most people display excitement with cheers, multiple guttural sounds and varied body exaggerations, Ed would seem to be unimpressed. Not so. Visual expression is not needed. An exploding of emotion happens in the mind and is no less impressive than displayed by others' animated expressions.

Expecting to catch a second glimpse of the elusive wolves Ed continued on the parallel trail leading to the beaver ponds. With the moist air the snow layer began to rot quickly. All tracks deteriorated to the point where old and new tracks deteriorated to the extent that old and new prints of rabbit, fox, squirrels and wolf blended.

Glad to be emerging from the wet bush Ed gave up expecting to cross paths with the ghosts of the woods. Sitting on a log at the water's edge Ed watched the sun rising. Sun rays penetrated the mist to wipe clean the air over the ice covered pond, a clearing of smudges from fogged eye glasses. Beavers would be sleeping in their huts after working the night shift. Fresh poplar tree limbs had been stacked in place at the hut mound on the edge of the pond. Disturbed water was ice free at the entrances to the submerged openings.

Though thin of thickness the ice lay mirror like without cracks on the stilled surface. Without winds to create waves it would not be expected to see the rise and fall of the ice in unison with the fluid composition of dark pond water. Yet, the surface moved by following the movement of an underwater creature. Beavers were asleep. If a lazy muskrat, it too would be sleeping; a tolerated boarder in a beaver hut. There were no fish of known existence in the ponds, at least not of a size to be able to create a force to move ice. Minnows existed and maybe a breed of carp though Ed had not seen any. Not being a fisherman; a wet line had never been tested in the pond waters.

A crack sounded from the middle of the pond and a dark nose popped up to suck in air. A slim sleek nose and snout appeared; distinctively different than that of the blunt nose and muscular jaw of the beaver. A long hump surfaced and dove revealing a long tapered tail. The sleekness of fur indicated the form of a freshwater otter. Not one but four heads popped up at different locations near shore. Three smaller heads continuously turned about when breaking the surface to keep in contact with the larger mother.

Ed sat motionless, even eyes stayed fixed in an open focus to take in a panoramic view. Letting the play and foraging take place without disturbance the otters displayed natural behaviours. Play was mixed with foraging though sibling fighting did occur over possession of foraging area or over a snail pulled from the depths of the mud. With conflicts soon forgotten the pups would play mutually with an empty snail shell until reminded by mother that constant foraging to sustain health is a priority. The pups gave a last toss of the shell before diving in search of a filled shell.

When fall turns to winter and the open water of Lake Superior begins to freeze from the shoreline out then fresh water otter head inland along the water veins of rivers and creeks to inland lakes and ponds. Easier access into ponds and warm marshes provides food supplies throughout the winter. Miles upon miles of waterways are highways of travel for the otter. Beneath the deep snow that occurs most of the time the earth does not freeze solid. An otter burrows beneath the snow and easily as a mole in search of grubs. Ed guessed that five miles of winding waterways had been travelled before the otter arrived to these ponds. Endless miles lay ahead further inland to be visited by the otter over the long winter.

Knowing that the otter were only passing through and would revisit on their spring return to warming lake waters, Ed remained frozen in position to watch the rascals at play for as long as possible. Disappointed by the brief encounter with the ghost wolves, Ed would absorb this otter encounter for as long as it played out.

With each increment of rise of the sun the less dense the mist became until disappearing and the surface ice began to dissolve. Ed welcomed the sun's warmth to dry wet clothing. His toque now covered only the crown of his head and gloves were discarded into pockets. When the bobbing of otter heads disappeared at the beaver dam, Ed stood, stretched and tuned to head home along the farm road. Pausing at a clearing just off shore of the pond Ed reminisced about an incident from a recent past.

12

Being single, a bit of a loner and having no spouse or children, so what is a man to do but carry out the functions of life alone. Chores around the farm are accomplished without assistance; at various times and without knowledge of any second person. Often concerned family members have stated, 'Do not do dangerous chores without someone being with you.' 'Let someone know when and where you are.' 'Carry a cell phone.' Talk is informative; filled with concern and meaningless.

People are concerned with their own lives and cannot be acquired at any old time at the whim of Ed's needs. Ed believed that at a current age of maturity he did not need to inform anyone of a daily schedule of constant location. Working a farm is a moment to moment change of location and chore. Having or using a cell phone is a waste of time; an invasion of the natural progression of enjoying life. According to Ed, cell phone use as a necessity and as an appendage is ridiculous and intrusive.

Standing in a clearing by the road, Ed recalled the fall day at this location where an incident occurred. Hindsight of concerned family members rang true; 'He should have had someone present.' 'Told someone of a time frame and location of the chore.' and 'Had a cell phone at hand for communication.'

A warm afternoon seemed fitting for the chore of cutting firewood, wood needed for warmth through the coming winter. The Stihl chainsaw was running well and chunks of log fell and stacked in two foot lengths. Sometimes the mind and body work independently and enjoy or suffer together or separately. Today the physical body worked in harmony with the chore at hand. It was the mind that was off kilter. On this day when weather and chore progression seem in sync, Ed's mind was in the ongoing sensation of a migraine.

Ed's body worked controlled by the mind's motivation section. The logic section of the mind lapsed, affected by the pulsating and electrical impulses of a migraine that can and does shut down the mind. A part of the mind seemed detached, able to be outside of the body and clearly view all happenings and be logical. Memories of past moments of life drifted in and out.

Then the accident that is unintended, unexpected, happens. Ed's mind clearly knew that the accident would happen and the cause. In slow motion ability a part of the mind viewed the incident from an out of body distance. Ed saw the tip of the bar and chain hit the butt end of a log and kick back. He knew what was going to happen. The migraine affected mind could not understand the pleas from the visual mind and could not instruct the body to react. The bar rose, his head turned, the thud of a strike to the chin echoed between ears and memories flashed. A whole life of events did not flash before Ed's eyes, though impressions of like incidents did in events of a past year and their links in a common thread.

Old Pacos was getting up there in years; considered to be in the senior seventies in human age. Not yet past its' prime, Pacos continued to work along with Ed skidding logs from the bush. From a perspective of an outsider, Pacos would be considered a dull witted gelding that moped about with laziness. The old boy may have resembled an unsatisfactory trophy horse to others, to Ed, Pacos was a thinking, strong worker that did not let trivial matters affect its' reserved demure.

No voiced working communication need occur between Ed and Pacos. Once harnessed for work Pacos took directions from the reins deftly handled by Ed. A light tap of reins to the rump to walk, a slight tug to stop, two tugs and back up. Once the reins slackened and were dropped Pacos drooped as if to snooze. Even muscles relaxed. Ed would wrap a chain around a log then clip a chain link into a hook on a draw bar. Hearing the sound is when Pacos twitched ears, lifted its' head and tensed neck muscles. When Ed picked up reins and taped the rump is when Pacos leaned into the restriction of the load. No prancing, no excitement, no balking and no resentment to the task at hand. Once the load is delivered and a trip made to the next load then Pacos would relax and doze. This is a smart thinking horse.

How would Pacos' patience be when put to the task of training a hyper young horse? On a spring day after the ground had dried sufficiently from winter, Ed harnessed Pacos and niece Cheyenne into a team harness. The reserves of Pacos and the gelding's mass would keep the young mare in check.

Though responding well to instructions, Cheyenne danced in place with hyper nerves and neighed to entice Pacos to get moving. True to form Pacos lowered its' head and relaxed. Ed fastened the chain to the log cascading butt end down the twenty-five foot slope to the creek bed. Cheyenne's ears constantly rotated, picking up every little sound from chain links clinking to crickets in the grass.

With a weary eye on Cheyenne's movements Ed carefully slipped a link into the draw bar hook with one hand and the other gripping the reins on the ground. Cheyenne lifted front legs and leaned against the collar and tense traces instead of leaning into the load with front hooves digging into the ground.

Holding position Pacos stood its' ground and waited for the reins to be lifted before reacting. Cheyenne was off balance with rear legs unable to move the load. The mare leaned into Pacos with enough bulk to push and topple the old boy to the ground. There it lay tangled in the harness and the weight of Cheyenne on top. Thinking it best not to struggle Pacos lay there being abused by a struggling and confused niece. What could the old boy be thinking, surely disappointed by the mare's actions, but reacting would just intensify the young horse's destructive movements.

Having the same temperament as Pacos, Ed moved slowly with a firm hold on Cheyenne's bridle and pulled downward to counter the tendency of a horse to rear up. The load would prevent Cheyenne from bolting while Ed disconnected the two harnesses to allow the mare to stand. Once standing, Cheyenne calmed enough to be unhitched from the whippletree. Free from the restraint the mare calmed and stood tethered to a tree. While in harness and wearing blinders on the bridle a horse cannot see to the rear. Now free to see, Cheyenne viewed the log, the slope to the gully and the aftermath of knocking Pacos over.

On the crest of the hill Pacos lay with its' back toward the recline at the edge. Though unhitched from the whippletree and reins and traces unhooked, Pacos could not roll up hill in order to stand. Ed's pull on the bridle only rocked head and neck. Not enough momentum would assist a Clydesdale's body to roll up hill. A horse on its' back will stop breathing. Knowing that Pacos was taking short breaths after long held breaths, Ed grabbed the underside back and front legs, lifted and pushed toward the creek below. One, two and three heaves and over rolled Pacos. Three complete rolls and a slide and Pacos arrived at the bank of a marsh of the creek bed.

Standing and shaking off the affects of rolling, Pacos surveyed the surroundings before walking along the creek edge to the road. Up the road, around the hill and back up the main road, Pacos returned to Ed, Cheyenne and the uncompleted job.

Showing disappointment, Pacos did not display any affects of the ordeal. Repeating the hook up of harness and attachment to the load,

Ed held reins tight and expected a replay of the previous attempt to drag the log. This time Pacos was aware and ready to counter Cheyenne's actions. Though Cheyenne pranced and jumped into the load, Pacos held the mare back and at the same time leaned into the harness to pull the dead weight of the log.

Over time the calmness and patience of Pacos taught the mare the art of working in harness. After training Cheyenne and Sierra, Pacos retired from work, turning over the work to the younger sisters.

Age is a state of mind, yet the body does not accept the mind's theory. Muscles decline, stamina decreases and the lustre attributed to youth fades to dull colours and bumps, scares and the telltale wrinkles of age. Pacos paid life's dues and deserved to relax and accept the fact that life can be lived at a leisured pace. Struggling to achieve this status has a down side; the inevitable fact that life will end. Though the odds of surviving to an advanced age have been successful up to this point, with each added year the odds increase the chances that death will happen.

In comparison, Pacos and Ed's Father were in the limelight of their lives. Dad at seventy five years of age was experiencing the ravages and effects of prostrate cancer. A decline in stamina increased and a waiting period unfolded. An end would arrive and the cure of fantasy thoughts would not happen. Miracles just do not occur when a person wishes.

Even when knowing the inevitable will unfold, life carries on, meals are prepared, laundry done and a day is lived. Knowing that a next day will arrive there are no plans made, no intentions and no expectations. Winter arrived as it does every year and the wonder of the Christmas season arrives with hope to be followed by the celebration of a new year. Dad was always the first to arrive at a family gathering and always the last to leave, despite Mother's hints of, 'It is time to go.' Weddings, birthday parties, reunions and even funerals, it did not matter; Dad was the last to leave. Was it the fact that he did not want the moment to end; the family to part, the sensation of laughter and human emotion to end?

An end is inevitable. What is intriguing is how events unfold in ways to assist a person with accepting and coping with life. Arriving at the farm after visiting Dad, Ed prepared to feed the animals. A fresh layer of snow covered the ground giving a virgin landscape over the mud, manure and discarded remnants of uneaten hay. Christmas day would be in three days and Dad was upbeat, an expectation of family gathering for a meal. Ed sensed something amiss, something did not seem right; in his mind turmoil lay over the farm in an upset aurora.

Usually the horses would greet Ed by approaching the hay barn. The cows and goats would gather at the hay feeder. Tonight they stood in place and waited for Ed to approach. Something was odd about the gathering. Mentally Ed counted heads, rhymed off names. A horse was missing. Counting again the number of horses did not add up, Pacos was not among the group.

Wild abstract thoughts form far fetched scenarios of stories. Ed's internal temperature rose and movement increased while eyes searched and a vocal call echoed through the crispness of cool night air. Hoof prints would be impossible to follow because of the fresh snowfall covering and filling in indents. Pacos had retained a white coat for the past five years. No longer did the gelding grow a golden coat in the warm weather months. If fallen down it would be difficult to spot white on white. Only dark eyes would stand out against the blur of white.

Neighing, a horse call, Ed hoped to call in Pacos if the horse was just out wandering. The other horses snorted lightly as if commenting among themselves. Their ears twitched, rotating in order to accept a distant reply. Pink noses on heads pointed in the same direction toward the back of the barn and trail to the north lower pasture. A low guttural reply bounced across the snow surface, just at the crest of the slope leading to the trail, Ed spotted Pacos' head straining to rise and look in the direction of the gathered.

Trudging forward, Ed feared the worst for the downed horse expecting a broken leg to be the worst of injuries and a certain need to end a horse's life. Not a natural end of a lived life. Maybe just a leg stuck in a mud hole of unfrozen earth beneath the soil?

Pacos lay with its' back towards the downward slope. Arriving, Ed passed hands over legs and joints, the neck and stomach and found no physical abnormality. Legs on the right side did not move, its' right ear, eyes and jaw seemed slack. Symptoms confirmed that Pacos had a stroke and crumpled into a restricted position.

The cause could only be speculated upon. If similar to heart strokes in humans then paralysis is usually on the left side of the body. Pacos' paralysis was on the right side. Could it be a stroke of some sort in the brain? Neither this cause nor a final diagnosis would be finalized.

Seeking assistance of brother Don, the men managed to roll Pacos up hill in order for the horse to lie in an upright position. Efforts to encourage the large gelding to stand were fruitless. Passing the hours of the evening with Pacos, Ed soothed the old friend, providing a blanket for warmth and affectionate caressing of ears and forehead.

Mourning was in a form of remembrance of past moments of their friendship together. Is it conceivable that Pacos understood and appreciated Ed's companionship at this moment when life drained from its' body? During the early hours of December twenty-third with its' head resting in Ed's lap, Pacos exhausted a last breath and tension escaped from its' body. Stillness prevailed before sounds of nature and barnyard life commenced.

On a farm, life and death is inevitable, births occur and deaths occur from a variety of causes. For Ed, emotion can vary from mild disappointment to lasting days of emotional despair. Pacos' death, due to the long years of companionship hit Ed hard at a time when Dad's illness fluctuated moment to moment.

With a house full of family on Christmas day, Dad rebounded, seemingly on a high only to be shattered days later when a down turn proved irreversible. With Pacos' passing, Ed had an introduction as to what would be experienced with Dad. Dad lay motionless in a hospital bed breathing with forced strenuous breaths, clinging to this world and not willingly wanting to leave any family member. Ed stood at the bedside, a hand upon the warmth of his hand until the last inhaled breath was not exhausted. All held their breaths; a silence prevailed, a moment of emptiness before hospital noises and human sounds continued.

Emotions erupted with the finality of life. Pain, hurt, anger, resentment and fear had been experienced throughout the two years of the progressing illness. A questionable relief was satisfied at the moment of death with the known fact that Dad no longer suffered pain and was at peace. In a quirky way he brought a final laugh to family members on New Years Eve, the night of his wake. When family members were last to leave the funeral home, Mother needed to visit the powder room.

Upon exiting she stated, 'Where's your Father? I always have to wait for him.' A scornful frown creased her lips.

Strange expressions and glances bounced between eyes of Mother's children.

'No Mother, Father is staying,' Ed said somewhat amused by Mother's words knowing exactly what mother was going to say next.

'Tesss,' Mother spurted between smirked lips forcing away the effects of mourning.

Relief laughter from the family filled the lobby of the funeral home, an odd sensation for a mournful place. Humour in remembrance brings the joy of a life lived. A combined sigh eased the tension of leaving the funeral home and leaving Father behind. Dad was always the last to leave a gathering and was last to leave his own wake and first ready for New Years Eve and never leave.

The instant fear of death compelled Ed to recall these memories at the moment the chainsaw bar punched into his chin and the spinning chain clawed down his neck and dug into the upper chest. As required the safety bar engaged to prevent the clutch from turning though the chain freely turned from assumed momentum with sufficient force to do damage. Enough kickback forced the chain through a leather coat and work shirt then digging deeply into the collar bone and chest muscles.

Ed reacted more to the force of the punch than to the cutting of flesh. An instant numbness that felt itchy occurred around the lacerations. 'Shit,' was all Ed said in reaction. Not yet knowing the extent of the lacerations, Ed did not panic nor go wild with emotion; a presentation often portrayed on film. He reacted logically and without worried anxiety. He was more pissed off with the fact that a day's work would be lost while seeking medical attention.

Placing the sputtering saw on the ground by the wood pile, Ed placed a hand over the ripped shirt and pressed against the wound. Walking to the truck and driver's side he leaned in through the open door and obtained a view of the injury in the visor's mirror. Removing the leather soaked glove, Ed was relieved to see no blood spurting; a good sign. Ripped flesh exposed pulsating veins and ragged strips of flesh. It would be a puzzle to sew the pieces together.

Placing the gloved hand against the chest and adding pressure, Ed decided to turn off the chainsaw, place it on the wood pile, close up the truck then drive back to the farm. Controlling the steering wheel with one hand the truck bounced over clay tracks and slipped through water filled ruts. Reaching the office building, Ed dialled 911 for assistance.

'Emergency service, how may I help?'

'I need an ambulance to my address.'

'Okay, what is the nature of the incident?'

'A chainsaw accident; a cut to the chin, neck and chest.'

'Are you in distress? I will stay on the line with you.'

'No, I will walk out to the road to meet the ambulance.'

'Is there anyone with you? It is best to stay on line.'

"No, I have a long driveway; they will not know where to go. Goodbye.'

'The ambulance will be there shortly. Is there anything further I can do?'

'I ain't got time to stay on the line and chit-chat,' Ed thought to himself as he began a long walk down the driveway to the main road. Wetness began to leach through the leather glove and chill against a warm hand.

Outside of the main social and industrial centre, living in the rural area means that the ambulance had to arrive from a neighbouring city centre. A matter of fifteen to twenty minutes would be the arrival time. The Township does have a volunteer fire department and a first response team made up of residents. Brother Don, living next door relished in being a volunteer and anxiously responded to the distress call relayed by the 911 dispatcher. Rushing to his vehicle, Don sped down the parallel driveway barely inches next to Ed's driveway entrance. Just the street name and lot fire number flashed in his mind. Don needed to rush to the number on the street that he also resided on. The number was familiar. Did he need to turn right or left?

Trying not to rush in order to maintain a calm pulse so that blood did not pump out of the wound with excess, Ed walked down the driveway. Eyes widened in bewilderment when seeing Don's truck speeding way. Yelling and waving the injured arm, both with restraint, Ed attempted to halt Don. Surely he would be searching for the fire number at a distance rather than the current number to his right at the end of the adjoining driveway entrance.

From across the road, neighbour Eugene noticed Ed at one extreme and Don in motion. Figuring out that something was amiss he waved arms in a stop motion to stop Don and pointed toward Ed further up the driveway. Realizing that the location was at this location a pale faced Don reversed and exited in first response.

Location and relationship to the injured victim stunned Don for a moment then training kicked in until a first repose unit arrived followed by the ambulance. The ride into town allowed moments of inactivity, a waiting period while the external vehicle sped to beat time. Emotion and welling moisture in Ed's eyes accompanied the contemplation of mortality. How close had he come to joining Dad and Pacos previously by less than a year? Rather than their passing it was the shared moments of life and incidents that Ed reflected upon. Dad could walk and often out walk Ed while out on hunting trips. It was Ed who often suggested taking a rest.

How close Ed came to a possible demise was not revealed until the injury to the chest was cleaned and the internal workings inspected. With colour of normalcy back in his face Don and the intern viewed the injury under the emergency room's concave light. Though the chainsaw cutting chain raggedly chewed up flesh and muscle it missed the main blood delivery artery by less that half an inch.

'What if' enters the thoughts at moments of danger and a new view of existence carries on with each new day. With forty odd internal and external stitches bringing most of the flesh together healing began and in a month Ed was back out cutting wood for the closing in winter, alone despite family stating cautious warnings.

13

Mom fell again and with expedient results the home care facility transferred her to the hospital emergency. Reaching eighty years of age is a milestone, though the travel through the years was not a smooth path. The past ten years being the most turbulent. Up to the point where Dad passed away, Mom was the strong, steadfast person. Taking care of finances and the home was unchanged, efficiently accomplished. The turnaround seemed to occur immediately in the first months of being a widow.

Surely the intricacies of health and mental functions had been accumulating over time with slight inflictions. Only in hindsight has Ed realized that the signs were there and that oddities with Mom's physical health and mental functions had taken a turn.

Math and its' multiple uses was child's play for Mom. Calculations were instant in Mom's mind, with no need to use pencil and paper or to tap pads on a calculator. Every aspect of running a financial home was in Mom's head down to the penny and at the end of a month the household budget balanced. Ed now assumed Mom's finances, his own disabilities in math requiring pencil and paper, calculator and multiple checking to accomplish what Mom once did in her head. Because Dad was gone, had Mom given up or had a health problem caused an inability to function.

Before calculators, before automated grocery store checkouts and debit cards, transactions were in cash and calculations of selecting priced objects required a mental capacity. Mom had that capacity . . . once.

Jumping back in time to a childhood memory, Ed visualizes an outing with Mom to a grocery store. Mom needed Ed, even at the age of seven, to push a second cart around the store. Having a house full of family and extended family members, groceries required would fill two carts. Mom had a list of food necessities in her mind and would wander up and down isles selecting required items.

While other patrons held lists and checked off the items and placed prices on the paper, Mom did not. No need; all selections and all prices were added, subtracted, multiplied and divided within her mind. Having only a fixed amount of cash on hand when reaching the checkout the amount of food prices needed to equal or be less than the amount of cash. Remember that back in the late nineteen fifties that there were no debit cards and cheques were seldom used so cash was the main currency. No barcodes for the cashier, no calculators for the patrons to use.

People would be embarrassed at the checkout when food items were recalled until a total equalled the patron's fixed amount of cash. This happened to people, though not to Mother. Mom was always accurate and if a discrepancy occurred she would challenge the ability of the cashier. When the frustrated cashier checked and double checked an error always surfaced. Ed was always amazed and was in awe of Mom's talent and ability. Even at a young age Ed knew that he lacked math ability though would not understand that the lack of ability was due to being dyslexic. For a kid watching his mother doing mental calculations was an ultimate magic trick with an anticipated ending of, 'will Mom's acquisitions add up to the cash on hand or will she be over, thus having the cashier having to recall items?' This never happened.

Mom picked up a can; two for a dollar ninety-nine, one for a dollar ten; a savings; four cans were put into the cart. A house-brand can be cheaper than a factory brand. Day old bread; four loafs at the same price of two daily fresh. Two cans of soup put into the cart; one can of caned tomatoes taken out. A constant adding and returning of items and Mom accurately kept track of a running amount.

Full carts arrived at the checkout counter where a wide-eyed girl tapped the cash-register keys blindly while eyes scanned price labels. Flowing from the cash-register's top a tickertape strip of blue printed numbers spat out. Click . . . click . . . click . . . whine, then silence until the girl sighed and ripped the paper strip from the exit slot. Taller than the girl the paper stretched from floor to her hand stretched at arms length above her head she folded it in half then in two fourths then in half again before handing it to Mom. Mom had handed the proper cash over and received a bit of change. Mom had done it again; had selected items, calculated prices and received change. 'Woo!' praised Ed, pushing a cart and following Mom out of the store.

'Wow!' thought Ed, 'that was a talent Mom had.'

Not anymore; Mom had fallen several times and always hitting her head against something to cause extensive bruising. This was not what caused the loss of mental capacity. Ed assumed that she had several strokes over an extended time frame; small strokes that had occurred which led to heart problems and eventually quadruple heart bypass.

To compound what a person may state is a big enough problem, dementia began to affect Mom's memory and physical abilities. Mom was always a strict Mother, not overly light-hearted or funny in Ed's or sibling's memory. Ed did notice changes in Mom's behaviour as dementia progressed; first, forgetfulness, and an inability to recall some mental functions of remembering telephone numbers and basic math. Then an angry phase emerged where she complained about incidents that occurred many years previously. Oh how she criticized what some people did or said forty years earlier and boy she would tell those so-and-so's off the next time they were encountered. Worst is a timeframe loss; in a sense past happy memories were current as if she were living the incident in the present. The unhappy aspect is that Ed had to inform Mother that an incident was in the past and that persons were no longer among the living.

Then the funny phase kicked in. Ed had never experienced the happy . . . comical . . . funny side of Mother. She laughed, smirked, made funny comments and recalled memories of a life that had joy, a life she experienced. Ed could only assume that this side of Mom's life occurred when out of sight of her children. After sixty years of being her child, Ed enjoyed Mother and the bonus, if one can call this phase of dementia a bonus.

What would the next phase exhibit? For the moment all was on hold while a last fall brought another strike to the head. More bruising occurred to turn the face black and blue and bordered by yellow rings. Just months after she turned eighty, when Ed was getting to enjoy a side of Mother unknown, physical accidents complicated her enjoyment of life.

Whether it be Mother or a farm animal, Ed worried about the well being of each. Caring for a person or a farm animal did not need to be questioned; immediate care is applied. When expecting the return of grazers at the end of the day, Ed counted heads. When all were accounted for, Ed's mind was at ease. If a single creature failed to be among the counted then various abstract scenarios flashed through Ed's mind. 'Wolves downed a goat; a fox lay claim to a duck; prowling bobcats were feasting on geese; a yearling was lost and unable to find its' way home.'

A young male goat thinking it was mature always lagged behind others, always the tardy one to bound out of the bush when the last glimmer of a setting sun's light flickered out. To counter the goat's tardiness Ed decided to call the herd in. All returned except the young billy. Sure enough; those abstract thoughts filled Ed's mind when repeated calls went unanswered then began the search through the bush, along the creek beds and marsh. Not one circuit but two then the start of a third. Loud baa . . . calls began to irritate Ed's vocal cords and a rattled call echoed on the cool evening air.

Goats mingled without concern, cows contently chewed their cud and Gertrude the Goose cocked a questioning head. Even the billy's mother seemed unconcerned about the absent kid. Frustrated with worry, Ed stood in the centre of the farmyard and gave a croaking baa . . . call. Directly in front of the round bail barn a prong horned head emerged from between rounds arching and stretching its back after a sound sleep.

Anxiety dissipated into relief and affection for Ed when the billy approached for a loving scratch on the head. Ed complied then also applied a side of the foot kick to the rump of the deceiving young billy.

Though the outcome in hindsight is comical and Ed could not hold lasting anger towards the billy, future tardiness would occur. Similar results would not be repeated when Babo the goat failed to return home. Knowing that the big mature goat could stand its' ground and defend the herd, Ed was not overly worried when various animals gathered for the evening feeding. Concerned fear began to tickle Ed's neck hairs when noticing that the goats would nibble on feed then wander to the trail leading to the lower north pasture. Something was wrong; they knew that Babo was late and knew it was not returning. Ed picked up on the odd behaviour of the goats and rushed down the trail, his eyes darting from side to side, wide eyes searching through the darkening landscape, searching for a goat form among the trees, undergrowth and un-burnt piles of brush.

Babo's black coat blended with the dark non-descript ground, its' white legs uncharacteristically stretched skyward and a white blazed forehead laying still. A fever of heat caused a cool sweat form beneath clothing as Ed rushed towards Babo with thoughts expecting death to greet him. Babo lay still; eyes slightly rolled back revelling the white of the orbs. Both front legs were pinched between the V of twin trunks of a dogwood tree. Obviously the situation was dire; blood flow in the legs not rising and tendons stretched beyond flexibility. Only a faint hiss of breath escaped a mouth that no longer strived for life.

Any animal lying on its' back for any length of time will give up living and stop breathing. Ed's instinct kicked in and he strained to lift the hundred and fifty pound goat. Barely lifting the weight off of the ground the legs would not escape the wedged grip. Turning Babo's head so that eyes viewed the world in normalcy, Ed ran back to the barn to retrieve a Swede saw. Glazed eyes of the goat watched Ed disappear into the dark, and thoughts of hope fading with sight.

With a last pull of the saw the smaller of the twin trunks cracked freeing stiff legs pinched at the knuckle of the hooves. Rolling Babo over, its' front legs remained stiffly straight. Ed gently massaged legs from the shoulder down, assisting the flow of blood. In the darkness of night after retrieving a lantern and blanket, Ed comforted Babo while slowly manipulating locked leg joints.

Once legs flexed and relaxed, Babo managed to curl them under its' body and lay in an upright position. Neither a sound of pain nor a sound of relief came from the lax mouth only a soft throaty purr. Offered water and sweet feed only touched lips. Ed placed both in front and placed a blanket over a damp body and sat with the old fellow late into the night. Just being there was and is important for the emotion of both parties. A connection transits species.

By early afternoon of the first day Babo was standing and by late evening when darkness began to eliminate shadows, Babo walked back to the barn. Both goats and cows watched the tedious painful walk that took the better part of an hour. All animals sensed the situation of Babo. Normally when feeding it is push and shove to see who would eat first and who would covet the most area. On this night the normalcy took place between goats and cows and the long legs of horses though all made room for Babo and they did not hinder the old goat.

Fall and winter played through, yet undoubtedly there was a change in Babo's makeup. The old fellow moved stiffly and when attempting to run it was more of a fast walk with front legs hopping straight legged. Rising on hind legs and playfully ramming Ed's hand no longer occurred. Ed would raise a flat hand and encourage playful contact. Having the instinct, Babo would waddle forward with head and neck and accept Ed's patting hand against its' forehead.

There was a change in the overall makeup of the goat. A spirit for life had been stifled by physical ability. Spring's warmth is always a welcome after a long cold winter. All animals stretch out and soak up the sun's warmth before the onslaught of hungry insects. Babo rested longer and longer each day as if practicing for old age and the end of life. Just by visual clues Ed knew that old age had arrived and it was just a matter of time before death arrived, and, it did.

On a day when all animals should have been grazing at various spots on the farm all hung around the front pasture near the duck pond. Green grass covered a high spot and there Babo laid down to accept the morning sun. Cows lay under the White Pine trees chewing their cud. Horses stood about randomly grazing on grass. Members of the goat herd lay in a scattered closeness to Babo. Even Gertrude and Heathcliff the geese lay close by.

Vanilla Goat, a young white female lay at the head area of Babo, just to be there. As the morning approached noon Vanilla laid her head upon Babo's neck. A silence seemed to linger over the farm. No baa . . . ing from goats; no neighing from the horses and countering by cows mooing. Even the geese held honking throats silent. A slow rise of Babo's chest told Ed that a last breath would be held before lungs relaxed with a silent escape of air.

At noon an odd sensation urged Ed to turn towards Babo. Silence encompassed the farm. Babo no longer took a breath. Lifting from Babo's neck, Vanilla lifted head and neck then rose and walked away. Following suit the herd of goats slowly wandered off to feed throughout the fields. Buttercup the cow approached and sniffed Babo before following No-Frills and calf behind the departing horses. Daily life continued on the farm.

Once the animals departed, Ed paid his respects to the old fellow and delivered Babo to a resting spot in the farmyard cemetery. Plots were beginning to add up. Babo lay beside Moglie Goat, in front of Ruff Dog and other neighbouring dogs come to rest.

Babo had a peaceful and respectful death, a rarity among animals in general. Humans have a better chance to experience a peaceful demise, though not always. Mother would not be so blessed. Abused by repeated falls had inflicted agony on her body and soul. Not wanting to be kept alive by artificial means nor to have extreme medical procedures that provide no guarantee, Mother had stated in-factually not to prolong the inevitable.

Falling into a coma does not allow family to say goodbye. Mother's body remained and functioned instinctively but her mind had left. Still, family gathered and talked, laughed and cried then laughed again as if communicating with Mother.

Each breath seemed mechanical, rising and falling after an extended hesitation. Mother lingered a day then two allowing all children to arrive along with her remaining siblings. As if satisfied to wait although absent Mother took a long held breath that did not exhale. With hands of family touching her warm hand Mother peacefully relaxed. Silence prevailed for a moment then the emotional tearing and crying of a life lost replaced the jovial reminiscing of Mother's life.

Living continues with memories of all of those gone previously and all will influence the living daily.

14

At a point in time in one's life, a person reflects on the past. There are many points in a life when reflection is contemplated. Ed had reflected on his childhood and the years growing up in a rural neighbourhood. Reflecting on farm life at this point has been a comparison between the lives of farm animals and family members and how both affect the other and how Ed has used one to deal and understand the other. Life is life regardless of creation distinction. There is a similarity and a comparison that can be made, but Ed will leave the philosophy up to the reader. Ed's reflection is only what has been visually observed and self analyzed.

Farm life is evolving and changing. Members live and die and new births rejuvenate the farm life. Memories will always be important and reflection through the mind is a history of farm life. Ed has taken a pause to reflect and create a file in his mind. At sixty-one years of age a new file is being created. Life on the farm will continue.

It was spring when Ed began reflecting and compiling incidents in life and what had transpired on the farm. Though death holds a significant and prominent place in the mind the wonders of life between birth and a final demise is filled with wonder, surprise, laughter and yes, all kinds of emotional love. This, we seem to forget when reminiscing and sometimes have to struggle to recall, but oh the joy when recalled.

Just when all seems stable and without a downfall Ed noticed Sierra's winter coat beginning to shed to reveal sunken hips. Ed passed a hand over the mare's chest and felt thinness over ribs. Age had crept up on Sierra and sister Cheyenne the daughters of Sanora and nieces of Pacos. A call to the vet for a check-up was not warranted, rather a cautionary inspection for Ed's peace of mind.

Almost twenty some years had passed when Sanorra was instantly killed by a lightning strike. Pacos followed sister Sanorra years later by stoke in the gelding's senior years. Dad had passed away that same Christmas week. Both had the same stanch presence with an easy acceptance of life. Buttermilk the mare Appaloosa, the mother figure of the herd died peacefully of old age one winter after the evening feed.

Tceque the Arabian-Quarter horse mare had expired strength and stamina when sucked chest deep in a creek bog. Food-Basic the cow lived a good long life, leaving a daughter, No-Frills to carry on the lineage of a Hereford-Charolais cross bread. Now, No-Frills shares farm calf production with a daughter, Buttercup, a large girl with Red Agnes lineage.

Moglie and Babo Goat, the bucks on the farm, have been joined by Fiona, Maggie-May and Vanilla for eternal rest in the Boot Hill Cemetery. A young generation of goats now roam the farm; Buster the head billy; Candy, Madge, Yvonne and Helga the does are busy rearing young.

Mother passed away in the warmth of summer as did Babo, Fiona, Maggie-May and Vanilla. Moglie, being different passed away in the cold of December of a hip dysplasia disorder.

Gertrude, despite her advanced age for a goose continues to raise wild goslings rescued by the humane society. At times the goose stands and stares over the farm as if searching for Heathcliff these years after the gander's passing. He had fought a distinguished battle against a bobcat, to protect other farm animals.

When having the vet out on a call it is best to check all residents. With a hopeful eye on the vet, Ed expected a positive nod, though not the case. Speculation that Sierra was just old thus the thinness and gaunt look was understandable. When checking Cheyenne who presented a healthy exterior, an internal inspection revealed a lump in the intestinal track, maybe a growing cyst or a tumour of cancer. Without performing extensive tests the cause could not be determined. Correcting the problem not recommended on an elderly mare.

As quick as the obstruction was observed it was within three days that Cheyenne died during a night's slumber. Had the sisters exchanged animalistic emotion within the dark? In the morning Ed first assumed that the large Clydesdale-Palomino-Hackney cross was sleeping peacefully under the warm morning sun. Sierra stood a short distance with face towards the sun. Sierra; the stubborn sister, the unaffectionate sister, the do not touch me sister for the first time in the years of association did not walk away when Ed approached. Ed raised a hand to caress the mare's nose. There was no backing away; instead the mare actually pressed a cool nose into Ed's hand. Ears did not press back, an indication of caution and flight. Perked ears tuned forward and allowed Ed to caress behind ears and eyes. After countless years of being anti-affectionate did Sierra feel alone and crave compassion . . . even from Ed.

In following days while Ed worked the farm, Sierra would actually seek out Ed and approach, expecting to be babied. This action is one hundred percent counter to the personality of the all white mare. The last equine on the farm must have felt lonely, neglected of a herd of fellowship. Tagging behind the cattle is an indignity to the breed of horses. Yet, follow the mare did to the dismay of Ed. The elder mare fell in the darkness of night when crossing the creek behind the leading cattle. A week after the passing of sister Cheyenne, Sierra's strength to stand lapsed after falling into the mud and sallow water and the mare's will to live dwindled.

The last farm horse was buried next in line of burial plots lining the fence bordering the chicken compound. A carved plaque listing name and dates was nailed to the fence post. An odd quietness prevailed over the farm. There were the normal, hectic sounds of farmyard critters, yet the smells and neighs of horses were missing in the musical score of animal sounds.

New chicks were born, turkey stock arrived, young goats played and four pigs took up home next to the goat house. Farm sounds continued and life expanded. In the early morning calm floats over the farm until Ed opens the first gate leading to the centre area. Gertrude honks first to let the others know of the master's arrival. In turn each animal greets and accepts feed and then goes about their day. Only the pigs squealed constantly until they receive their slop mix. Gertrude stomps into the goat portion of the barn and gives the pigs a verbal scolding, as if to say, 'quit complaining, you will be fed, wait your turn.' Having a say, Gertrude waddles away to associate with accommodating and social farm residents; eating beside goats, snoozing with the cows and chattering with chickens clucking complaints about crowing roasters.

Slopping up their feed the pigs settle down and have a morning nap in order to digest blotted stomachs. Quiet will prevail until the evening feed. Farm life continues and evolves. Memories a pleasant reflection while Ed relaxes on a hay bail and leans against a fence rail to reminisce.

THE END

OTHER TITLES AVAILABLE FROM
MOOSE HIDE BOOKS
Imprint of
MOOSE ENTERPRISE BOOK AND THEATRE PLAY PUBLISHING
Visit our web site at www.moosehidebooks.com For complete title listings.

HISTORY – BIOGRAPHY
    Local Hero (Volume One)
    Out of the Gutter
    A Long Exciting Trip to Peace
    An American Trapped in a Communist Paradise
    Lingering Impressions
    The Long Way Home
    Roosevelt Street
    Reflection

www.ingramcontent.com/pod-product-compliance
Lightning Source LLC
Chambersburg PA
CBHW022111050726

47591CB00002B/754